THE VALUE OF LEARNING: FROM RETURN ON INVESTMENT TO RETURN ON EXPECTATION

Valerie Anderson

The Chartered Institute of Personnel and Development is the leading publisher of books and reports for personnel and training professionals, students, and all those concerned with the effective management and development of people at work.
For full details of all our titles, please contact the Publishing Department:
Tel: 020 8612 6204
E-mail: publish@cipd.co.uk

To view and purchase all CIPD titles:
www.cipd.co.uk

For details of CIPD research projects:
www.cipd.co.uk/research

THE VALUE OF LEARNING: FROM RETURN ON INVESTMENT TO RETURN ON EXPECTATION

Valerie Anderson

UNIVERSITY OF PORTSMOUTH BUSINESS SCHOOL

© Chartered Institute of Personnel and Development 2007

All rights reserved. No part of this publication may be reproduced, stored in an information storage and retrieval system, or transmitted in any form or by any means, electronic, mechanical, photocopying, recording or otherwise without written permission of the Chartered Institute of Personnel and Development, 151 The Broadway, London SW19 1JQ

First published 2007
Reprinted 2008 (twice)

Cover and text design by Sutchinda Rangsi-Thompson
Typeset by Curran Publishing Services
Printed in Great Britain by Short Run Press

British Library Cataloguing in Publication Data
A catalogue record for this book is available from the British Library

ISBN-13 978 1 84398 196 1

Chartered Institute of Personnel and Development
151 The Broadway, London SW19 1JQ

Tel: 020 8612 6200
Website: www.cipd.co.uk

Incorporated by Royal Charter. Registered charity no. 1079797.

CONTENTS

	Acknowledgements	vi
	List of figures and tables	vii
	Foreword	viii
	Executive summary	ix
1	**Value and evaluation: the context**	1
2	**Value and evaluation: influencing factors**	7
3	**Value for whom?**	11
4	**Alignment**	19
5	**Measuring and reporting**	29
6	**Conclusions and implications**	39

Appendices

A	The research project	43
B	Online poll results and summaries	47
C	Examples of measurement options	51
	References	55

ACKNOWLEDGEMENTS

The CIPD would like to thank the members of the University of Portsmouth research team responsible for conducting the Value of Learning project, Dr Valerie Anderson, Prof Charlotte Rayner and Simon Turner.

We would like to express our gratitude to all those who were prepared to share their time, experiences and ideas with us, through participating in the online discussion thread or responding to online polls. Particular thanks go to those individuals and organisations who participated in the interview process: Canon UK and Ireland, Christian Aid, Clifford Chance, Dublin City Council, The Football Association, Glasgow Housing Association, The Innovation Group plc, Lyreco UK Ltd, the National Audit Office, Schaeffler (UK) Ltd, Tesco.com and VT plc.

Additional thanks go to Janice Caplan, CIPD Vice-President (Learning, Training and Development), and her panel of experts for their advice and guidance.

LIST OF FIGURES AND TABLES

Figure 1:	Training to learning	2
Figure 2:	Characteristics of a strategic approach to value and evaluation	4
Figure 3:	The value and evaluation process for strategic LTD	4
Figure 4:	The Partnership Model	12
Figure 5:	The alignment process	27
Figure 6:	A model of value and evaluation	40
Table 1:	Senior managers' and LTD executives' views on strategic readiness	13
Table 2:	Senior managers' and LTD executives' views on LTD investment decisions	21
Table 3:	Senior managers' and LTD executives' views on benchmark measures	32
Table 4:	Approaches to assessing the learning value contribution	38
Table A1:	Semi-structured interviews: participating organisations	45
Table A2:	Poll results of first online poll	48
Table A3:	Poll results of second online poll	49

FOREWORD

All of us who are involved in learning, training and development are displaying a great deal of energy and confidence. The acquisition of both individual and team knowledge and skills is recognised as essential to organisational success. One consequence is that our professional skills are increasingly valued.

However, if we are to grasp the opportunity we must adopt a new mind-set and develop new techniques. Models developed in the third quarter of the last century are no longer appropriate. This report considers one particular area where change is needed: how we should measure and report on the value of learning. This has become a central feature of the management of learning; it should not be solely about the impact of a training initiative, still less about justifying the role of the training department. We must focus on the needs of the organisation and the learner. Trainers can no longer regard their activities as the sun around which learner planets revolve.

The research outlined in this report has been undertaken on behalf of the CIPD by the University of Portsmouth. The approach they have adopted is disarmingly simple: dual interviews were undertaken in 12 organisations. An identical set of questions about the strategic value of learning and its measurement were put to a senior member of the operational team and the most senior person in the learning, training and development function. A comparison between the results offered considerable insights on the role of learning, training and development; these insights extended way beyond those concerned solely with measurement and reporting. This dual interview approach was initially developed by the ASTD (American Society for Training and Development) and we are most grateful to them for allowing us to reproduce their questions.

Similar differences in perspective between the senior operational managers and the learning professionals were reported in both the ASTD and the CIPD studies. Most importantly, there is a need to focus on the initial alignment of the learning interventions with the organisational strategy. Get that right and the choice of ways of measuring and reporting becomes much clearer. What the Portsmouth researchers have done is to identify the factors that should be taken into account when determining the appropriate measures. They have produced an indicative list of the metrics that could be used; they have articulated a clear process that can be used to determine the ones that are relevant to the reader's organisation.

One size does not fit all. The development and implementation of an appropriate strategy requires thought and effort in the context of the particular organisation. As a result the conclusions may not find favour with those seeking a simple template to apply irrespective of the circumstances. Still less will they find favour with those who develop and market such templates. To quote the US writer Upton Sinclair: 'It is difficult to get a man to understand something when his salary depends upon his not understanding it.'

However for the great majority of training and learning professionals, who are committed to developing modern practice, this research is welcome and timely. We are grateful to the team from the University of Portsmouth for the thoroughness with which they have carried out their task. We are very pleased with the resulting output and commend this report to the profession.

Martyn Sloman, Adviser, Learning, Training and Development, CIPD, August 2007.

EXECUTIVE SUMMARY

Learning is now a strategic issue for organisations. This report explores how organisations are measuring and reporting on the contribution of learning to strategic value. It highlights the need to build on and move beyond traditional approaches to training evaluation and offers a new model of value and evaluation. The report argues that learning practitioners should move away from a 'one size fits all' approach to evaluation. It is the value expectations of stakeholders that should inform the choice of measures used to report on the contribution that learning makes to the organisation.

The report draws on data gathered from learning, training and development (LTD) practitioners and senior operational managers in 12 UK-based organisations.

The research shows how key organisational stakeholders expect learning to add value. Such value is delivered through contributing to infrastructure effectiveness and through the achievement of strategic differentiation. The research also demonstrates that, while some direct correlation of the LTD contribution and 'the bottom line' is possible, learning also contributes to longer-term and less tangible organisational outcomes.

Traditional approaches to training evaluation advocate a series of levels to assess the effects of individual learning and training activities. These levels take into account learners' reactions to the learning experience, the learning achievements of participants, changes in their job behaviour and the organisational effect of specific learning interventions. There is abundant evidence, however, that applying traditional evaluation approaches to strategic learning processes may be problematic. In particular, traditional approaches to evaluation set out to prove the merit of specific learning interventions and to demonstrate their cost-effective delivery. Such proof, however, while identifying that the trainer has done good work, does not necessarily assess the extent of the alignment of the training intervention with the organisation's strategic priorities. The developing role of the LTD professional and the requirement for a more strategic contribution requires a new approach to value and evaluation.

The research shows that most organisations still have some way to go with the development of appropriate measures. However, the following four factors influence the way that learning is valued:

- senior management trust in the learning contribution
- organisational requirement for learning value metrics
- the strategic significance of short-term capability requirements
- the strategic significance of long-term capability requirements.

This report explores the alignment of learning processes with organisational priorities. Strategic priorities change over time and learning activities are funded through a variety of different budgets. Therefore, constructive dialogue with organisational stakeholders is essential. Alignment, like strategic evaluation, is both an outcome and a process.

Both the challenges and opportunities for measuring and reporting on the value of learning are considered. Qualitative as well as quantitative assessments of the value of learning are needed and four main approaches to measuring and reporting on value are identified:

- learning function efficiency measures
- key performance indicators and benchmark measures
- return on investment measures
- return on expectation measures.

The research identifies two important trends. First, measures of performance against key performance indicators and benchmarks are frequently used to assess the strategic value of learning. Second, very few organisations find return on investment metrics to be appropriate as a strategic measure of the value of learning. Instead, return on expectation measures, which make use of both 'hard' numerical and 'soft' qualitative information, are more effective. It is this second trend, the move from return on investment to return on expectation, that offers the most exciting opportunity for the LTD professionals of the future to demonstrate their value to the organisation.

The report is based on a study undertaken for CIPD by researchers from the University of Portsmouth Business School. The study built on and developed a research process established by researchers at the American Society of Training and Development (ASTD) in 2005.

VALUE AND EVALUATION: THE CONTEXT   1

- **Learning is now a strategic issue for organisations, and a strategic approach to evaluation is required.**

- **This must focus on the value expectations of key organisational stakeholders rather than the functional preferences of training practitioners.**

- **The approach must be grounded in the alignment of learning processes with the organisation's strategic priorities.**

- **It must identify the value expectations of stakeholders in order to inform the choice of reporting measures.**

INTRODUCTION

A clear link between effective HR processes and organisational performance has now been established through research undertaken in USA and UK (Huselid et al 1997; Pfeffer 1998). Research (Purcell et al 2003) has highlighted the importance of effective HR processes in ensuring that employees have ability and skills, motivation and incentive, and opportunities to participate in their work environment. It has also highlighted the important role of effective line management in the achievement of discretionary behaviour leading to performance outcomes (CIPD 2007b).

Those responsible for organisational performance in the UK as elsewhere are increasingly aware that sustainability and productivity depend on the capability of their people at individual, team and organisational levels. This presents many opportunities for the learning, training and development (LTD) function but poses new challenges relating to the need to align learning processes with strategic priorities and to analyse, measure and evaluate the value contribution that learning is making.

This chapter outlines the context for the CIPD Value of Learning project and the way that the research was carried out.

LEARNING AS A STRATEGIC ISSUE

Over many decades learning and training professionals have set about designing, delivering and evaluating a range of interventions to enable people to learn new skills and perform tasks in a more effective way. Organisations have recognised the benefits of encouraging and facilitating the development of all or some of their people, enabling them to identify and develop their potential for the longer-term benefit of the organisation (Bryans and Smith 2000).

As organisations have recognised the knowledge-intensive nature of their competitive environment, the importance of learning rather than training has been increasingly accepted. Whereas training tends to focus on skill-based behaviours delivered through content-based and instructor-led interventions, learning is a broader concept involving the acquisition and application of knowledge, skills or attitudes that result from formal or informal development, education or training experiences.

Learning is, therefore, more self-directed, adaptive and work-based (Sloman 2007) and surveys confirm that although instructor-led training (in its many forms) is helpful, work-based learning is consistently rated as more useful by both employers and employees (CIPD 2005b, 2007a). Increasingly, therefore, there has been a requirement to develop work-based learning opportunities in addition to the provision of task-focused training interventions. This is illustrated in Figure 1.

The change in emphasis from training to a broader concern for learning to foster individual and organisational performance has significant consequences for the role of LTD practitioners. The focus on instructor-led and content-based interventions that underpin a primary concern with training has been replaced with the requirement for practitioners to facilitate a range of different forms and opportunities for learning. The primary concern with the value of the training experience for trainees has also been replaced with the need to focus on the value benefits of learning processes for the department and/or organisation as a whole. As a result practitioners have had to foster and develop new relationships between the learning function and the wider HR and management community (CIPD 2005a).

The move from training to learning has occurred as the new paradigm for human resource managers and developers has focused attention on a more strategic role. They are urged to become 'business partners' (Huselid et al 1997; Purcell et al 2003; Ulrich

THE CONTEXT

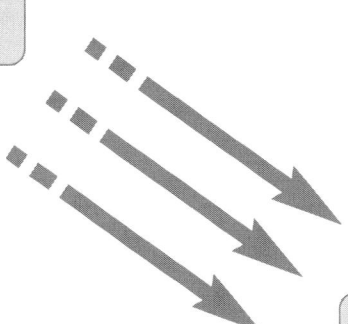

Figure 1 Training to learning

Training
An *instructor-led, content-based* intervention, leading to desired changes in behaviour

Learning
A *self-directed, work-based* process, leading to increased adaptive potential

Source: CIPD 2005a.

and Brockbank 2005). Within this approach, LTD professionals are encouraged to influence strategic decision-making processes, to ensure that learning and training processes are aligned with the strategic priorities of the organisation and to demonstrate the contribution that learning can make to business success.

Empirical evidence, however, suggests that the strategic potential of learning has yet to be realised in many UK organisations. Survey data from UK learning and training managers indicates that only one-third feel that LTD implications are taken into account when overall organisational strategy is discussed and formulated; it also shows that the LTD function is not a key stakeholder for organisational strategy in almost half of organisations (CIPD 2007a). Survey data from the USA has similarly indicated that less than 20 per cent of chief executive officers (CEOs) were very satisfied with the level of alignment of LTD with business goals (Accenture 2004).

A STRATEGIC APPROACH

Many LTD professionals will, of course, continue to operate outside the strategic arena, and many senior decision-makers will remain unaware or unconvinced of the contribution that learning makes to the development of the organisation's human capital. This issue is increasingly being addressed through national and organisational interest in human capital measurement and reporting. Insights from this area are highly relevant to the development of a more strategic approach to valuing learning.

Human capital comprises the knowledge, skills and experience of the organisation's people. An economically based concept of human capital as an important organisational and national asset has been established for many years (see, for example, Becker 1964; Schultz 1961). Organisations and governments alike now recognise that human capital and people development is an important part of organisational strategy and performance (Fitz-Enz 2000).

Such features as knowledge, skills and experience, of course, reside in individuals rather than the organisation (Scarborough and Elias 2002). A key requirement for organisations, therefore, is to invest in the growth and development of the knowledge, skills and experience of individuals but also to foster and enable a 'conversion process' such that individually held human capital assets become part of the organisation's collective 'intellectual capital'. In this way the organisation can develop and deliver products and services that have market value (CIPD 2006c).

Learning and training are key to this value creation process. Investment in learning provides the basis for the development of the organisation's human capital assets, and learning processes also enable the conversion of those individual assets for the benefit of the organisation through the development of the organisation's, culture, values and processes.

In its broadest sense, evaluation involves determining the worth, value or merit of learning and training. The CIPD fact-sheet on training evaluation (Thomson 2007) points out that evaluation has always formed an important part of the role of professionals in learning and training. The difficulty of measuring learning, which may not be manifested or applied in practice for a period of time after any intervention, has long been recognised. The change in emphasis from time-defined training interventions to work-based learning processes undertaken over a less-defined period of time presents further challenges.

Recent thinking about evaluation and about the contribution of LTD to organisational performance has also highlighted the extent to which assessments of 'value', 'worth' and 'merit' are dependant on their context. Ulrich and Brockbank (2005, p11) point out that: 'Value is defined by the receivers of HR work – the investors, customers, line managers, and employers – more than by the givers.' 'Value', therefore, is defined by the receiver of something, rather than its 'producer'. It is important to note that, within organisations, different stakeholders may well have different perceptions of the value of learning. It is one thing to ascertain the value or worth of a learning intervention to the learner; it is another to assess its value to management (Nickols 2005; O'Driscoll 2005).

A more strategically orientated approach to human resource management (HRM) and LTD, therefore, requires a review of the purpose of evaluation, the data that may be gathered and the timing of evaluation activities. When considered against this strategic perspective, traditional hierarchical evaluation may be too limited and a fresh approach is required. (See Box 1 for a summary of the issues relating to traditional hierarchical evaluation.)

The developing role of the LTD professional and the requirement for a more strategic contribution, therefore, requires a new approach to value and evaluation and this is illustrated in Figure 2.

SOME KEY ISSUES

Figure 2 indicates that any framework of value and evaluation requires an assessment of the current alignment of learning and training processes against the organisation's strategic priorities. From the LTD professional's perspective there are two aspects to this process. First, working with management decision-makers to assess strategic learning priorities, and second, ensuring that learning investments and processes are aligned with those priorities.

Current thinking about value has also indicated that different organisational stakeholders may perceive the value contribution that learning makes in different ways. Therefore it is necessary to concentrate less on data relating to the experiences of learners and trainers. Instead a focus on the expectations of departmental managers and the organisation as a whole is required, based on relationships with a range of organisational stakeholders. A further issue for LTD professionals is to understand what expectations different stakeholders have for learning, and for this to inform the choice of measures that are used.

These key issues of alignment and establishing a range of relevant and organisationally appropriate measures are illustrated in Figure 3

THE RESEARCH PROJECT

Against this background the CIPD appointed members of the University of Portsmouth Business School in November 2006 to undertake the Value of Learning research project. The research was exploratory in purpose, aiming to establish how practitioners

---

BOX 1: LIMITATIONS OF TRADITIONAL APPROACHES TO EVALUATION

Most traditional approaches to training evaluation (see for example, Kirkpatrick 1975; Bramley 2003) have advocated a series of levels through which to assess the effects of individual learning and training activities. These levels take into account: learners' reactions to the learning experience, the learning achievements of participants, changes in their job behaviour and the organisational effect of specific learning interventions. Some practitioners (see, for example, Kearns 2005) have also suggested a calculation process to determine the economic return on investment (ROI) for learning and training interventions.

There is evidence, however, that applying traditional evaluation approaches to strategic learning processes may be problematic. UK survey data (CIPD 2006a) has suggested that only one-third of UK organisations seek to capture the effect of learning on the 'bottom line' and 80 per cent of LTD practitioners believe that learning delivers more value to their organisation than they are able to demonstrate. Data from USA has also suggested that these difficulties are not confined to UK organisations (Sugrue and Kim 2004). A number of factors may explain why, in practice, there are problems with implementing traditional approaches to evaluation.

First, there may be problems with the purpose of evaluation activities. Traditional approaches to evaluation set out to prove the merit of specific learning interventions and to demonstrate their cost-effective delivery. Such proof, however, while identifying that the trainer has done good work, does not necessarily assess the extent of the alignment of the training intervention with the organisation's strategic priorities. A more strategic approach to evaluation, therefore, would focus more on assessing and improving the contribution of a range of learning processes to organisational priorities as they emerge (Thomson 2007).

Second, there are issues with time-orientation. Traditional approaches to training evaluation can only look backwards at what has been achieved to determine the effectiveness of programmes that have taken place, an approach sometimes referred to as a 'summative' process (Russ-Eft and Preskill 2001). O'Driscoll (2005) and Dionne (1996) both point out that a strategic approach to evaluation requires a more forward-looking assessment of the contribution learning is currently making and might make in the future to improve the productivity and sustainability of the enterprise (a 'formative' approach).

A further difficulty is with the nature of the data collected. A strategic approach to management and performance is integrative and concerned with the collective effect of interrelated factors that underpin organisational performance and value creation. As such senior managers are not concerned about detailed attempts to directly attribute cause and effect relationships to any one particular organisational variable (or training intervention). Whereas a traditional approach to evaluation focuses on the reactions and consequences for learners and trainers resulting from discrete and individual learning interventions, a strategic approach requires a focus on the aggregate value contribution made by a more dispersed range of learning processes.

Figure 2 · Characteristics of a strategic approach to value and evaluation

Traditional evaluation approaches

Focus on
- individual learning interventions
- learner and trainer perspective
- specific learning measures
- measuring trainer effectiveness
- proving the value of LTD activities

→

Strategic approaches to value and evaluation

Focus on
- strategic organisational learning processes
- organisational perspective
- aggregate organisational data
- measuring the effectiveness of learning processes
- improving LTD contribution to strategic goals

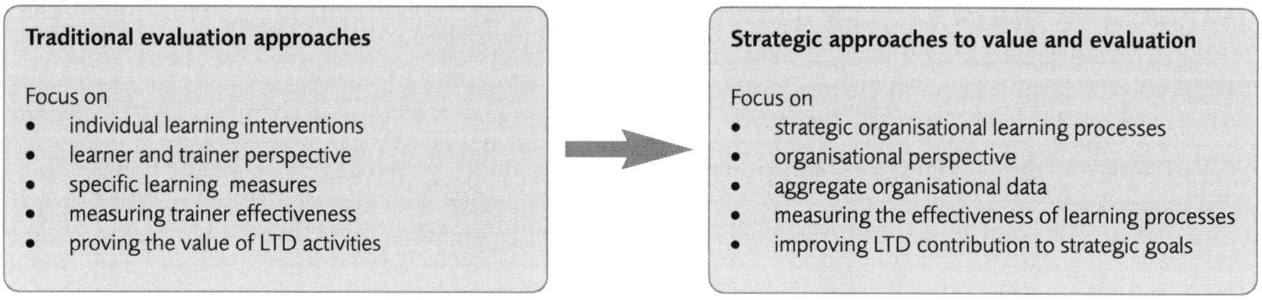

Figure 3 · The value and evaluation process for strategic LTD

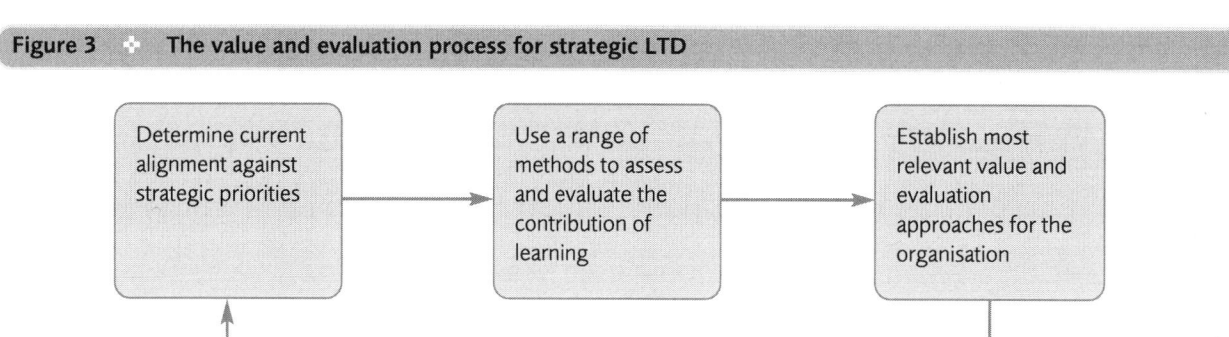

Determine current alignment against strategic priorities → Use a range of methods to assess and evaluate the contribution of learning → Establish most relevant value and evaluation approaches for the organisation

and senior decision-makers perceive the value of learning, and how organisations are measuring and demonstrating its strategic value to the organisation as a whole.

The CIPD research was influenced, and built upon, an important research project that was undertaken by the American Society for Training and Development (ASTD) in 2005 (Sugrue et al 2006). There the researchers undertook a number of semi-structured interviews within large private sector organisations. This enabled them to comment on the extent of alignment between the LTD function's perceptions of the value contribution made by learning and the perceptions of senior operational managers.

The CIPD research sought to build on and extend this approach in order to enable a fuller examination of features relevant to the value and evaluation process as it is developing in UK organisations. A fuller description of the research process is provided in Appendix A; however, as with the ASTD study, the heart of the approach involved a series of two separate interviews. In total 24 semi-structured interviews were undertaken in 12 organisations. They were designed to find out how learning and non-learning stakeholders perceive the value of learning. Separate interviews were held with a senior operational or business manager from the organisation and with the most senior person responsible for LTD. Although interviews were conducted separately, the same interview questions were asked of the senior manager and the LTD executive.

Whereas the ASTD study focused on large private sector organisations, the sample of organisations for the CIPD research included companies of different sizes and types.

The interview questionnaire used in the CIPD study is reproduced in Box 2. The first six questions are identical with those used in the earlier ASTD study and we are grateful to them for their permission to allow us to proceed in this way. Gathering the different perspectives from the operational managers and LTD professionals by conducting separate interviews using the same questions provided considerable insights. We would recommend and advocate that LTD professionals consider using this approach themselves in their organisations.

As well as the information gained from the semi-structured interviews with operational and learning managers at executive level in the 12 organisations, the CIPD study also included information gathered from LTD professionals operating in a range of different roles and levels. This was achieved through inviting practitioner contributions to an online discussion thread about issues, challenges and practices relating to the value and evaluation of learning and training and through two online polls for practitioners (see Appendix B).

REPORT STRUCTURE

The information gained from the organisational interviews on seven questions set out in Box 2 will be presented in the central body of the report. Case study illustrations drawn from the 12 organisations will be used throughout, as will data from the organisational interviews, the online polls and extracts from the online discussion thread. The report is structured as follows:

BOX 2: VALUE OF LEARNING INTERVIEW QUESTIONS

QUESTION 1: How does the learning function provide strategic value to your organisation?

QUESTION 2: How will the learning function's strategic activity translate into business results?

QUESTION 3: What is the learning investment process and your involvement in it?

QUESTION 4: How do you know the learning function is maintaining ongoing alignment with your organisation's strategic business needs?

QUESTION 5: How do you measure the learning function's value contribution to your organisation today?

QUESTION 6: How do you know that the learning function is functioning as efficiently as possible?

QUESTION 7: Measuring and reporting on value:

a) Please could you describe any form of benchmarking or 'scorecard' measurement that you undertake here regarding learning and development? (If so, what measures are used?)
b) What challenges and opportunities do the benchmarking or scorecard approaches to measurement provide for you? (and why?)
c) How meaningful is the benchmarking or scorecard data for senior managers? (and why?).

- *Chapter 2* addresses different factors that affect the way learning is valued and the choices that organisations make to identify how best to measure and report on the value that learning brings to the organisation. It demonstrates that LTD practitioners must develop the approach that is most suited to the particular circumstances of their organisation.

- *Chapter 3* considers the different perspectives of value that are attached to learning in different types of organisations, and the expectations different stakeholders have of the learning contribution. The information from Questions 1 and 2 in Box 2 will be considered here. The chapter shows that some direct correlation of the LTD value contribution to the 'bottom line' is possible but that an awareness of the longer-term and less tangible value of learning is also necessary.

- *Chapter 4* discusses the particular issues related to alignment. It highlights how alignment is a process as much as an outcome because strategic priorities develop and change over time. The information from Questions 3 and 4 will be considered here.

- *Chapter 5* focuses on the issues of measuring and reporting on value. The information from Questions 5, 6 and 7 will be reviewed. Four different approaches to measuring and reporting will be identified. The chapter highlights a shift from concern with return on investment approaches to one focused more on return on expectations.

- *Chapter 6* presents a new model of value and evaluation and assesses the implications of the model for LTD practitioners.

VALUE AND EVALUATION: INFLUENCING FACTORS

2

❖ **The way that learning is valued will be affected by four main factors:**

   – **senior management trust in the learning contribution**
   – **organisational requirement for learning value metrics**
   – **strategic significance of short-term capability requirements**
   – **strategic significance of long-term capability requirements.**

❖ **These factors are not mutually exclusive and LTD practitioners should take them all into account.**

❖ **Some factors will be more significant than others. This will depend on the context of the organisation.**

INTRODUCTION

This chapter examines the different factors that affect the way learning is valued. The factors were identified in the course of the semi-structured interview process and supplemented with information from the online polls and the discussion thread (see Appendices A and B).

SENIOR MANAGEMENT TRUST IN THE LEARNING CONTRIBUTION

In responding to the interview questions many of the interviewees reflected on the extent to which a level of trust in the contribution of learning was evident in their organisation. Two issues became evident. First, there were varying levels of trust in the contribution of learning in different organisations. This trust may result from the prior views of senior managers about learning or may be the result of recognition of good work being undertaken by the learning function. Second, LTD executives were well aware of the need to foster and sustain trust in learning through building relationships with key decision-makers and line managers in different parts of the organisation.

The following case illustration highlights the importance of fostering and maintaining trust in a not-for-profit organisation.

CASE ILLUSTRATION

Christian Aid

Christian Aid is an international relief and development agency. Its essential purpose is to work with partner organisations to 'expose the scandal of poverty, contribute to its eradication, and to challenge structures and systems that keep people excluded'. Its Chief Executive, Daleep Mukarji, highlighted how learning forms part of the way the organisation operates, indicating that: 'The learning function infiltrates the whole of the organisation. It makes us understand how we can get better and how we can be having greater impact and influence.'

The Head of Learning and Development, Jimmy Naudi, also reflected on the issue of trust and the implications of this for the contribution that the LTD function offers to the organisation. 'I think I must be riding on a key number of individuals within the organisation that believe that learning and development is a positive thing for the organisation to do. ... I can pinpoint within this group a number of key people who would sponsor, so to speak, learning and development.'

In addition Jimmy Naudi focused on the need to build and maintain a trust-based reputation: 'I'm also riding on the reputation that we have within the organisation so I'm very keen that once we promise something it gets pushed through to completion'.

The online poll data complements this illustration (see Appendix B). The data indicated that 81 per cent of respondents agreed with the proposition that: 'Senior managers will be less concerned about value of learning metrics if they have developed a relationship of trust with the LTD function.'

ORGANISATIONAL REQUIREMENT FOR LEARNING VALUE METRICS

The interview feedback relating to requirements for learning value metrics suggested that high levels of trust in the learning contribution may also be accompanied by a strong requirement for learning value metrics.

All but three of the 12 organisations described some degree of requirement for corporate measures of learning effectiveness. Moreover, high expectation for such measures is not confined to those organisations which benefited less from senior management trust. Two particular features of the requirement for metrics are evident in the data. First, the use of 'up-front' metrics in making a justification for investment in LTD. Second, an acceptance, by both LTD practitioners and senior line managers, of the multidimensional nature of organisational metrics and the difficulties this poses.

The following case illustration concerns an organisation where there are high levels of management trust in the learning contribution as well as a high requirement for learning value metrics.

CASE ILLUSTRATION

Tesco.com

Tesco plc is one of the world's leading international retailers and Tesco.com operates as a 'business within a business' to drive forward its online retail processes in the UK. Around 1,500 people work for Tesco.com, which is the most successful online grocery shopping service in the world. Operational efficiency and a decision-making process grounded in consideration of the business case is fundamental. Laura Wade-Gery, Chief Executive of Tesco.com, expressed it like this: 'In general we would very rarely embark on something where we couldn't see [or] ... be able to build a business case.'

Metrics are part of the way of life in LTD as elsewhere. However, the focus is on multidimensional and aggregate measures that have strategic relevance to the business. Laura Wade-Gery explained how the Tesco 'steering wheel', as a form of balanced scorecard (Kaplan and Norton 1992), forms the basis for measurement and decision-making: 'What I'm looking for is consistent improvement in that steering wheel, year on year. Continuing improvements year on year. And I don't, if I'm honest, spend a lot of time saying, "well, if we spend x on training, which of these measures will it hit?" It's a slightly more intuitive process that says, "okay, if I'm back to my consistent theme of trying to grow sales by x per cent, therefore you can quite see that reducing staff turnover is only going to be a good thing."'

At Tesco.com, therefore, the management requirement for learning value metrics complements senior management trust in the learning contribution. For example, for a significant investment in an ongoing management and leadership development programme, Therese Procter, the Personnel Director, explained that the senior management team were prepared to trust in the process and the investment without a full 'up-front' business case. Laura Wade-Gery reflected on this decision in this way: 'What I've got is, I suppose, a belief that by producing managers/leaders who are that much more capable of doing things through others, we end up standing a better chance of getting what we need done.' As a result, the investment 'was given a big tick without a financial return on investment'.

Metrics, therefore, are an important way to communicate the contribution that LTD is making but may not be sufficient on their own. The online poll results (see Appendix B) confirm this and suggest that only a minority of respondents (38 per cent) 'would like my organisation to rely on metrics to determine the value of learning'.

SHORT-TERM LEARNING CONTRIBUTION AND CAPABILITY REQUIREMENTS

Interviewees from all but three of the 12 organisations highlighted the important contribution learning makes to meeting short-term capability requirements. There is no simple 'cut-off' point between short-term capability and long-term capability as these are defined in different organisational contexts. However, two themes became evident.

First, learning is expected to contribute to continuous process and productivity improvements. Second, it is expected to enable minimum 'time to competence' for new skill areas in addition to continuous updating. This was particularly important for those organisations where specialist skills form a major part of their competitive offering. Some illustrations from the case organisations are set out below.

BOX 3: SHORT-TERM PERFORMANCE REQUIREMENTS

VT plc

A key contribution of learning, 'is around raising all employees' performance by a couple of notches' (Jo Robbins, HR Director).

The Innovation Group

'It comes down to the productivity piece. Because I've got to deliver certain aspects of software to certain points at certain points in time. I need productivity to be as best it can' (Shaun Gwilliam, Software Solutions Director).

'When we've got new people coming through, specifically, the training role I deliver, when it's our new people, ... they come out and they're making an impact as soon as possible. ... They've got to learn the products and then they go in and then they'll be given tasks. You ... want them to complete them credibly and accurately and yet in as fast [a time] as possible' (Steve Morey, Training Officer).

Clifford Chance

'Strategically what we are trying to achieve is to give our people the skills to work more effectively so they give better client service at the end of the day. [We] add value by giving them those skills' (Julia Clarke, Global Learning and Development Partner).

'The basic business concept of this firm, and any other large-scale law firm would be the ability to sell the mental aptitude of the individual lawyers. It's their ability to be as up to date as possible, both in terms of the law and of the surrounding environment in which they're working for business issues that determines their ability to add value. So strategically, they have to keep ahead, ideally, and at least abreast of, everything that's happening developmentally. And ... the competency goes ... one step further: that's to learn how to apply it in a business advisory function' (Stuart Popham, Senior Partner).

The National Audit Office

'The learning function ... is really responsible for providing the backbone of skills and capabilities of the individuals doing, delivering the work that we do and that is the strategic value' (Julian Wood, Director of Development and Employment).

'If we didn't train people to those professional standards we would ultimately not be able, as it were, to practice. So it's absolutely fundamental to the sort of organisation we are. That is in a way one of our comparative advantages, our ... key selling point: that we do have that professional knowledge and experience highly concentrated in the organisation' (Tim Burr, Deputy Comptroller and Auditor General).

To different extents, therefore, the contribution of learning to meet short-term capability requirements is important for organisations. The interviews also highlighted an expectation that learning would contribute toward longer-term capability requirements.

LONG-TERM LEARNING CONTRIBUTION AND CAPABILITY REQUIREMENTS.

All but one of the 12 organisations referred, in the semi-structured interviews, to the expectation that learning would help meet the long-term capability needs of the organisation. Half of the organisations highlighted the importance of investing in learning to underpin talent and/or management development but other issues were also discussed. Three of the organisations, for example, highlighted the importance of investing in learning to ensure that the skills and behaviours needed for the future would be in place. A further two organisations also highlighted how learning investment was important to foster an appropriate 'change-orientation' amongst employees at all levels. The case illustration below highlights how these factors are important for a public sector organisation.

CASE ILLUSTRATION

Dublin City Council

Dublin City Council is the largest local authority in the Irish Republic and one of the biggest employers in the city. As well as planning and economic development, it manages housing, environmental services, refuse collection, water, roads and streets, and the fire brigade.

Local government in Ireland has been coping with a sustained change process since the mid-1990s following a national government initiative, 'Better Local Government'. Maire Twomey, Training Manager, indicated the contribution learning makes to the long-term capability issues that this involves. First:

> helping staff to deal with that change, helping them to address that change. I think a well trained staff, a staff who are given development opportunities will be more flexible and better equipped. Generally speaking they are a better equipped workforce. I think what we are trying to do here is give staff opportunities to learn new skills for their current roles but also very much focusing on their own development which would benefit both themselves and the organisation in the future.

Second, as part of the contribution to building a skills base for future needs, Dublin City Council has invested in a major 'upskilling' and ongoing development process for all staff in the organisation:

> It's around the organisational capability to meet the expectations of key stakeholders. One of the key actions in this part of the business plan is to promote and offer a range of learning opportunities to our workforce from literacy and numeracy, for those who need it right through to third level education.

Third, Dublin City Council has also focused learning investment into developing management and leadership capability:

> We are looking at management and management capabilities, and we're very conscious of developing current capabilities but we are also looking towards the future and developing capabilities for the future of the organisation. ... It encourages people to think outside the box and ultimately there is a benefit to the organisation in terms of providing good management skills for the future.

The interviews suggest that in some organisations the highest priority is given to the development of short-term capability. In others the primary focus is on long-term capability. For many of the organisations participating in the research, however, both long-term and short-term capability is important.

The online poll provided an opportunity to probe these issues (see Appendix B). It included a proposition about the relationship between short-term and longer-term capability issues and a proposition about 'all staff' development opportunities. Although only two of the interviewed organisations highlighted investment in 'all staff' development priorities, fewer than 40 per cent of the LTD respondents to the poll agreed with the proposition that 'investment in learning in the organisation should be focused on achieving job-related competence rather than developing individuals' potential'. There was, however, a strong level of agreement (82 per cent) with the proposition that 'Balancing the need to invest learning resources in addressing short-term issues as well as longer-term learning needs is a challenge in my organisation'.

Online poll data, therefore, suggest that LTD practitioners may value 'all staff' development opportunities more than their line management colleagues. However, it also confirms that they are aware of the need to balance priorities related to longer and shorter-term priorities.

CONCLUSION

This chapter has highlighted some important differences in organisational expectations of learning and in the factors that may affect the way learning is valued and evaluated. These factors (trust in the learning contribution, requirement for metrics, long-term capability requirement and short-term capability requirement) are not mutually exclusive. LTD practitioners should always take them all into account. Depending on the particular context of the organisation, some will be more significant than others. The next chapter probes further into the contextual nature of 'value' to examine what different stakeholders in different organisations expect from learning.

VALUE FOR WHOM? 3

- **Learning, training and development will only be perceived as successful if organisational decision-makers believe it produces value.**

- **Decision-makers expect learning to contribute to strategic differentiation as well as to the operational infrastructure of their organisation.**

- **Some direct correlation of the LTD contribution and 'the bottom line' is possible, but awareness of the longer-term and less tangible value of learning is also necessary.**

INTRODUCTION

This chapter examines the issue of 'value' in more depth. It considers the feedback from the first two questions asked in the semi-structured interviews:

- How does the learning function provide strategic value to your organisation?

- How will the learning function's strategic activity translate into business results?

The discussion builds on the issues raised in Chapter 1 (see pages 2–3) in relation to the contextual nature of the concept of 'value'. Determining the value of something depends on the perspective of its 'receiver'. Value is, therefore, an individual matter and so assessing the worth or value of learning will involve asking the question 'It's value for whom?' A particularly well-received perspective on this topic has been offered by Ulrich and Brockbank and is summarised in Box 4.

HOW THE LEARNING FUNCTION PROVIDES STRATEGIC VALUE

Within organisations there are a range of different people or groups (stakeholders) who have an interest in the outcome of learning and training activities. This has emerged in ongoing CIPD research projects and has been summarised as the Partnership Model (see Figure 4).

BOX 4: A STAKEHOLDER PERSPECTIVE

The requirement for HRM practitioners to focus on the needs and expectations of both external and internal stakeholders has been identified by Ulrich and Brockbank (2005) as part of what they term the 'HR value proposition'. They identified five elements that underpin the HR value proposition for any organisation:

- knowledge of external business realities

- meeting the needs of external and internal stakeholders

- crafting appropriate HR practices

- building HR resources

- assuring HR professionalism.

From this perspective, learning and training will only be perceived by the organisation as being successful if its stakeholders believe that it produces value.

Figure 4 The Partnership Model

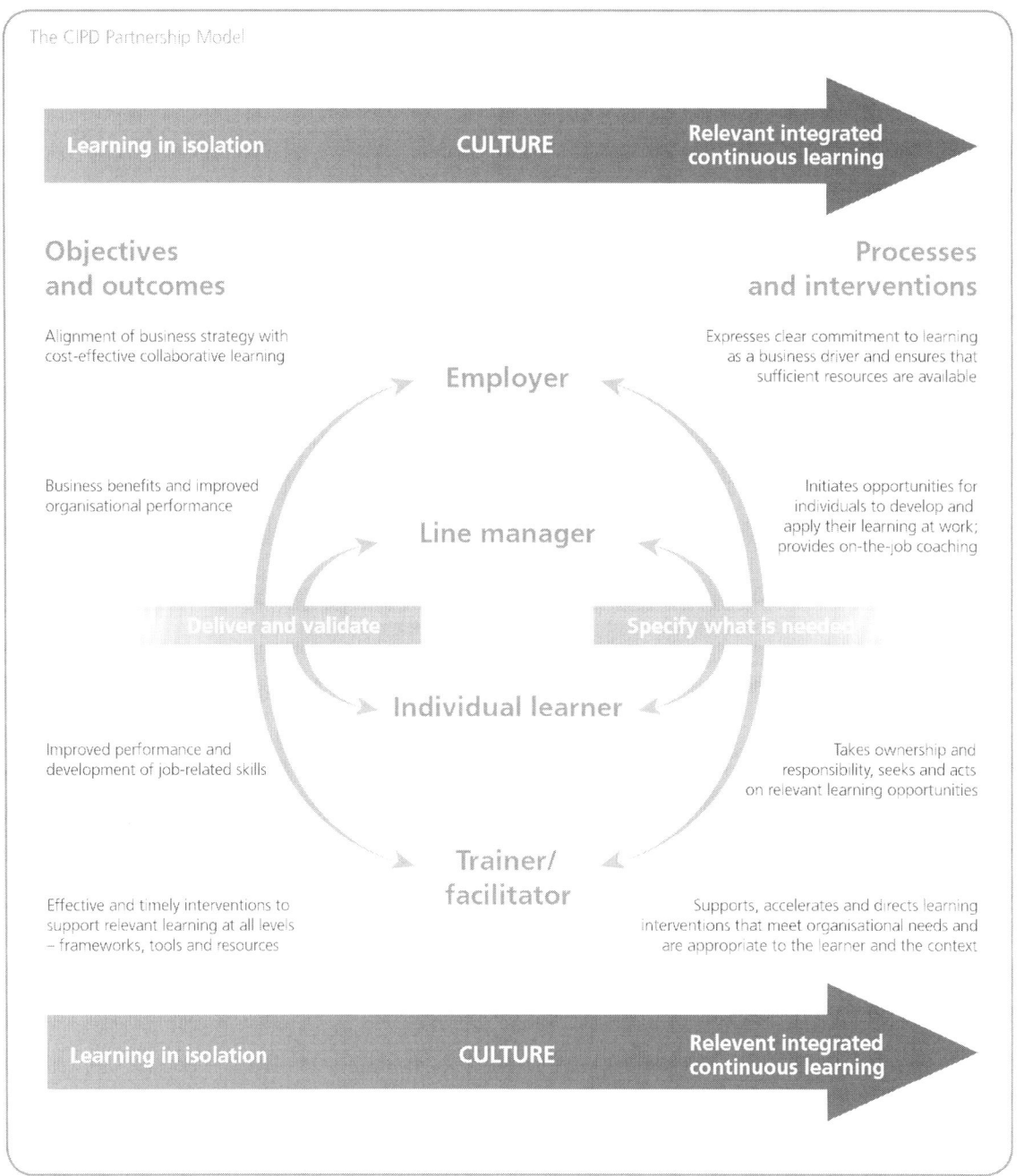

Source: CIPD 2006b.

Although different stakeholders have an interest in LTD outcomes, traditional approaches to training evaluation involve measuring the value of learning for trainees and this process is instigated and undertaken from the trainer's perspective. Other organisational stakeholders, in particular line managers and senior management, have found traditional evaluation approaches to be less relevant as there has been little attempt to clarify the extent to which learning makes a valued business contribution (see Chapter 1).

Therefore, the semi-structured interviews set out to explore how the 'learning value proposition' is perceived both by senior managers and by LTD executives. The first question asked in all these face-to-face interviews was:

> How does the learning function provide strategic value to your organisation?

The responses to this question highlighted four main ways in which senior LTD practitioners and senior managers perceived a value contribution:

- ensuring the strategic readiness of employees
- delivering performance improvement
- delivering cost-effective labour
- enabling career/talent management.

By conducting separate interviews but using the same questions it was possible to identify some similarities and differences that arose between the senior-manager and LTD-practitioner 'constituencies'. Both senior managers and LTD executives highlighted the importance of learning for the strategic readiness of employees and the importance of delivering cost-effective labour. However, LTD executives were more likely than senior managers to highlight the career/talent-management value contribution of learning. The senior managers as a group, by contrast, were more likely to focus on the important contribution of learning to performance improvement issues.

Some overlap between the issues was apparent from the interviews, and three of the issues are considered more fully here to illustrate and consider both the similarities and the differences in perspective of the senior managers and the LTD executives. These issues are:

- strategic readiness of employees (highlighted equally by LTD executives and senior managers)
- performance improvement (highlighted more by senior managers)
- career/talent management (highlighted more by LTD executives).

Strategic readiness

The expectation that learning will contribute to the strategic readiness of employees was most frequently mentioned in responses to the first question in the semi-structured interviews. This is particularly true in the responses from private sector organisations. The quotations in Table 1 illustrate some of the comments made.

Performance improvement

The expectation that learning will contribute value through performance improvement was mentioned more by the senior managers in the interviews than by their LTD colleagues. The responses suggest that it is an important value contribution for all types of organisations (not-for-profit, public and private sectors). There were, however, some differences in the nature of the performance improvements that were mentioned by the interviewees.

Table 1 ❖ Senior managers' and LTD executives' views on strategic readiness

	Senior manager	LTD executive
Canon UK and Ireland	'Learning and development [contributes] ... both at management and senior management levels to develop our future European leaders, but also at a skill based level to provide sales training where it crosses across Europe, particularly in some of our new market ventures' (Matthew Norton, Channel Director).	'But it's very much also about preparing for the future. ... What does that mean for the jobs, and skills and behaviours that we need of our people going forward?' (Caroline Price, Strategic Business Partner, HR).
Lyreco	'For me, in logistics, in the whole company, it's all about training people to meet the future needs of the business' (Alistair Wood, Logistics Director).	'In terms of strategic intent, we realised that as the business has grown, we have responded to the different needs of customers within the business and you have got big operational departments like field sales, corporate accounts, different aspects of logistics and they have all wanted different things' (Ian Lawson, Training and Development Director).
VT Group	'Obviously it's no good having strategic intent if you don't understand what's going on out there in the marketplace. ... One of the things we've done, for example, we've given all of our top graduates the job of analysing our competition and they present to us as a Board, where those competitors are going compared with where we believe we're going in the same marketplace. ... So they learn a lot on the job, we learn from them' (Paul Lester, CEO).	'That says it all really. Out of the six objectives ... four are building for the future' (Jo Robbins, HR Director).

A minority of interviewees focused their responses on the learning value contribution of improving performance levels generally. Paul Lester, CEO of VT Group plc, for example, commented that: 'if we could improve everybody's performance by broadly 10 per cent then we'd have a hell of a company on our hands.' More often, however, interviewees focused on the contribution learning can make to enhance management and supervisory performance. The quotations in Box 5 illustrate the main points made here.

Career/talent management

If the value of learning for improving performance is perceived as particularly important by senior managers, the value of learning for talent development was perceived as particularly important by the LTD executives.

In half of the 12 organisations, interviewees reflected on the value contribution made by learning through career/talent-management processes. It was most commonly observed by those working in larger organisations. The quotations in Box 6 illustrate this theme.

EXPECTATIONS ABOUT THE LEARNING VALUE CONTRIBUTION

The insights about the value of learning gained from the face-to-face interviews provide an opportunity to consider the wider expectations of senior people. Traditional approaches to the evaluation of training and development tend to focus on the contribution learning makes to operational efficiency and to the quality enhancement of product or service delivery (Thomson 2007). The articulation of a more strategic focus to learning and development, however, focuses attention on the potential to contribute to the achievement of strategic differentiation by the organisation.

Building on the work of Purcell et al (2003) the CIPD has highlighted the need for HR professionals generally to ensure delivery of both:

- competent, efficient and effective operational infrastructure processes

- strategic differentiation through a bundled framework of processes to support innovation and creativity, commitment and engagement, learning and competence, all of which are positively aligned to the organisation's 'big idea' (Johns 2005).

Evidence from the Value of Learning project highlights how senior decision-makers do indeed expect learning to contribute both to operational infrastructure processes and to strategic differentiation. Cost-effective labour and performance improvement contributions, for example, add value to the effective operation of the organisation's infrastructure. In addition, learning is expected to add value to strategic

---

BOX 5: LEARNING VALUE CONTRIBUTION THROUGH ENHANCED MANAGEMENT PERFORMANCE

The Football Association

'Now why is that a strategic value? Because the company helps their [management] staff to do their job better, feel better about themselves, about their abilities, about their dedication to the company, and in return they are better equipped to get better at doing their job, which I think is an objective of a manager year on year, to help their staff get better at what they do' (Simon Johnson, Director of Corporate Affairs).

Lyreco

'There were lost phone calls, there were very long response times on the phone, productivity was fairly flat, sickness wasn't great and staff turnover was very high. ... We put together a programme purely for the team leaders and they all went through that and almost the next month you started to see all kind of changes in the results' (Ian Lawson, Training and Development Director).

The National Audit Office

'We're trying to make the organisation more effective in achieving its goals. But we have in the last few years very much overhauled our approach to the learning of management skills' (Tim Burr, Deputy Comptroller and Auditor General).

Dublin City Council

'In terms of actually dealing with poor performance it's very difficult. ... Coming out of that it was recognised that there was a real deficit in management capacity and capability' (Kathy Quinn, Head of Finance).

BOX 6: CAREER/TALENT MANAGEMENT

Dublin City Council

'While our training and development programmes look at the skills staff need for their current jobs, they also encourage staff to look at their development in terms of a career within the council. We are looking at people who still, by and large, come in to the Council to have a lifetime career and that can span a number of years – up to and in excess of 40 years for some staff' (Maire Twomey, Training Manager).

Lyreco

'The other one which we've developed over the past couple of years is to pick out the rising stars, and to give them a career development workshop. ... We're really looking [at] one or two promotion steps beyond where they are [and] finding out what they're good at' (Alistair Wood, Logistics Director).

VT Group

'In terms of the effective deployment of the most talented. I mean, we had a project team and the project team worked on what we meant by talent and what we wanted to do with talent and they produced a policy document and a process to use to manage talent' (Jo Robbins, HR Director).

---

differentiation. This is achieved by contributing to the strategic readiness of employees and to effective career/talent-management processes.

Contemporary thinking about strategic HRM places most emphasis on the requirement for strategic differentiation. However, analysis of the interviews for this research illustrates the overlap, in practice, between strategic and operational infrastructure processes. Performance improvement, for example, was referred to by interviewees as a matter of operational efficiency and as being of strategic significance. It involves both general performance improvement (operational infrastructure) and enhanced management and leadership performance (seen as a strategic differentiator).

The following case illustration indicates how learning contributes to strategic differentiation in a UK-based office supplies organisation.

CASE ILLUSTRATION

Lyreco UK

Lyreco UK is part of a large family-owned office supplies group operating extensively in Europe, Canada and Asia. In the UK the business is run from the head office and distribution centre in Telford where, each day, 15,000 orders are processed, and 60,000 parcels are picked, packed and despatched across the UK for next-day delivery. The customer promise is 'Yours tomorrow or yours free'. In the office supplies market Lyreco are currently number two, and it is no secret that they have ambitions to be the biggest and the best.

The distribution market is highly competitive and Lyreco are convinced of the strategic value of effective people development and learning strategies to underpin the growth of the business. Alistair Wood, the Logistics Director cites a connection between sales and profit metrics and the organisation's investment in developing people to meet the future needs of the business.

In the words of Ian Lawson, Training and Development Director, 'You are only as good as the people you have got. ... You need the people to deliver the results'. Developing leaders and teams, and becoming an employer of choice, therefore, have been key components in the drive to increase market share. This strategic approach to leadership development has underpinned the development and promotion of people from within the organisation, so that 50 of the 55 UK area sales managers have been developed internally and 23 of the 24 distribution centre supervisors have also been grown internally.

The interviews with senior managers and LTD executives indicated that learning can make a value contribution in two main ways: first, through ensuring operational efficiency, and second, through contributing to strategic differentiation. However the value contribution is achieved, it is also important to consider how it is linked to the organisation's 'bottom line'. This is considered in the next section.

HOW DOES LEARNING LINK WITH BUSINESS RESULTS?

The second question asked in all the semi-structured interviews was:

> How will the learning function's strategic activity translate into business results?

In the CIPD research interviews, the responses of both senior managers and LTD executives on the learning contribution to business results were very similar. Interviewees in nearly all organisations highlighted how learning linked directly to the achievement of some of the organisation's key performance indicators (KPIs). In addition they highlighted less tangible, but nonetheless relevant, business outcomes from the learning contribution. While there may be a place for simple economic 'translations' of value expectations to short-term, quantifiable bottom-line benefits, therefore, this may not always be appropriate and an appreciation of the value of less quantifiable benefits is also necessary.

It is important to distinguish here between 'metrics' and KPIs. Key performance indicators are specific metrics relating to performance in activities that are critical to the success of an enterprise. While an organisation may utilise a range of metrics, its KPIs will focus on those things that are of *fundamental importance* ('make or break') to organisational success or failure. As such KPIs can provide an indication, now and for the future, of organisational performance in areas where that performance can be quantified and managed. In addition to a focus on core financial indicators of performance, many organisations have now identified other operational KPIs that are crucial for success; these will differ depending on the different circumstances of each organisation.

KPI monitoring enables managers to spot and correct weaknesses in the organisation, and so it is not surprising that such measures were referred to in the Value of Learning interviews. In particular five areas of KPI were highlighted in the interviews: customer satisfaction levels, talent retention, service quality delivery, sales targets and sales margins, and productivity levels.

In addition to these tangible business measures, interviewees highlighted the effect of the learning function's activity on organisational capability. A range of different capabilities were identified. Nearly all interviewees reflected on the contribution made by learning through 'ongoing general capability development'. Here there was an expectation of value through initial skills development, by diminishing the time to competence, as well as value through ongoing capability development. The quotations in Box 7 illustrate this point.

In addition to general and specific-skill-related capability development, interviewees from a third of the organisations also highlighted how learning contributes value through the development of management capability.

When reflecting on this sort of contribution, senior managers and LTD executives commented on the inappropriateness of a simple translation of these benefits to short-term 'bottom-line results'. This point was also made by some of the LTD practitioner-contributors to the CIPD value of learning online discussion thread that formed a part of the research process (see Appendix A) as the extract in Box 8 illustrates.

BOX 7: BOTTOM LINE CONTRIBUTION BY LEARNING TO ORGANISATIONAL CAPABILITY

Clifford Chance

'What it [learning] is doing for the business is that it's ensuring that we are guiding people as to how to develop the skills that we need them to develop for the business. We've identified what skills for business we need for them to be effective. More than effective – excellent at what they do' (Julia Clarke, Global Learning and Development Partner, Clifford Chance).

Dublin City Council

'Another of our objectives in the business plan would be to develop organisational capability to meet the expectations of all the stakeholders through the implementation of HR strategies' (Maire Twomey, Training Manager, Dublin City Council).

BOX 8: VALUE AND THE BOTTOM LINE

'The value to the organisation should be considered in much broader terms. For example, the longer term benefit from staff who are change-friendly, the reputational value of having qualified staff, the value of embedded organisational learning (rather than just individual learning) and the impact on talent acquisition and retention. These are no easier to measure in hard financial terms than most other outcomes but they may be of value. ... Like many other forms of investment, you sometimes have to speculate to accumulate' (Graham O'Connell, contributor to the CIPD value of learning discussion thread on 15 December 2006).

The same point was made by many of those participating in the semi-structured interviews, but they were nonetheless confident of the business benefits of less tangible and more general contributions. The quotations in Box 9 illustrate this point.

CONCLUSION

This assessment of the perceptions of the value of learning held by senior managers and LTD executives, therefore, highlights two key points:

- Learning is expected to contribute value to the organisation through:
  - enabling the organisation to develop and maintain an effective operational infrastructure
  - contributing to strategic differentiation by ensuring the strategic readiness of employees, management and leadership development and effective career/talent-management processes.

- Decision-makers are aware of the contribution that learning makes to organisational KPIs, but are also aware and appreciative of the less tangible, longer-term value benefits that learning can deliver.

BOX 9: THE ECONOMIC VALUE OF LESS TANGIBLE LEARNING CONTRIBUTIONS

Dublin City Council

'One of the key actions in the business plan is to promote and offer a range of learning opportunities to our workforce through literacy and numeracy ... [and] if you go to the other end of the spectrum we are looking at management capabilities. We're very conscious of developing current capabilities but we are also looking towards the future and developing capabilities for the future of the organisation' (Maire Twomey, Training Manager, Dublin City Council).

The Football Association

'If you have a well-performing workforce, then you're going to deliver better. Your overall targets of the business will improve. It's quite difficult to track that, but that's the focus of it really' (Tom Harlow, Learning and Development Manager, The Football Association).

Canon UK and Ireland

'When we talent manage effectively we save money directly on recruiting and generate value by someone being able to go faster earlier' (Matthew Norton, Channel Director, Canon UK and Ireland).

Schaeffler

'I think that it all goes back to the bottom line. It's impact on productivity; it's impact on absenteeism and it impacts certainly on the morale of the organisation which is very important for motivation. ... These soft issues actually come straight through onto the hard measurements. It's something where we always thought there would be a direct connection ... but some of the stuff we were doing was 'leap of faith' stuff ... and it was nice to see the results actually coming through (Roger Evans, Plant Director).

ALIGNMENT   4

* **Learning involves a range of organisational stakeholders, and learning activities are often funded through a variety of different budgets.**

* **Effective learning requires agreement to invest in the time needed to learn as well as financial support.**

* **Some organisations find internal key performance indicators to be helpful in the assessment of alignment to specific organisational priorities.**

* **Other organisations use external benchmark measures to ensure ongoing alignment to longer-term skills and capability requirements.**

INTRODUCTION

This chapter discusses the complex process of alignment. How can LTD professionals facilitate learning interventions that are aligned to the strategic priorities of the organisation? The chapter reviews feedback from the third and fourth questions asked in the semi-structured interviews:

* What is the learning investment process and your involvement with it?

* How do you know the learning function is maintaining ongoing alignment with your organisation's strategic business needs?

Clearly, at a strategic level, learning will not be valued or valuable unless it is targeted on outcomes that make a difference to issues that are significant to the organisation (Burrow and Berardinelli 2003; Sadler-Smith et al 1999; Phillips 1998).

Any strategic framework of value and evaluation, therefore, requires an assessment of the current alignment, 'fit', linkage or integration of learning and training processes with the strategic priorities of the organisation. First, it is necessary to assess the extent to which any initial investment in learning is aligned with the organisation's strategic learning priorities. Second, it is important to ensure the ongoing alignment of learning processes with strategic priorities.

ALIGNING THE LEARNING INVESTMENT PROCESS

Alignment is an integral feature of a strategic approach to LTD; however it is under-researched. Not much is known about how alignment is achieved in organisations and the ways in which it can be measured. These issues were explored in the semi-structured research interviews with senior managers and with LTD executives, and the results are considered here.

The third question asked in all the face-to-face interviews was:

> What is the learning investment process and your involvement with it?

The responses highlighted the complex and fluid nature of learning investment processes. Training and learning processes are funded through a variety of different budgets in organisations. Finding the time and space needed for learning can be just as important as agreeing a financial investment, and the size of the organisation itself may influence perceptions of the nature of the learning investment as the illustrations in Box 10 show.

The interviews highlighted how, in most organisations, different aspects of learning are funded through a variety of different budgets – and that these may be the responsibility of different people. Some budgets are managed by LTD or HRM practitioners; other sources of funding are the responsibility of other stakeholders who may or may not be positive towards learning. These sources are not necessarily designated for LTD purposes. These points are illustrated by the quotations in Box 11.

These quotations illustrate how alignment requires LTD practitioners to convince others in the organisation to invest in learning through budgets held outside the training and learning function. This will be achieved only if those stakeholders believe

> **BOX 10: INVESTING IN TIME TO LEARN**
>
> While financial investment is important, an equally challenging issue highlighted by senior managers is the challenge of the investment of time needed for learning. The following quotations, all from senior managers, illustrate this point:
>
> ### Clifford Chance
>
> 'Within reason we actually spend as much as we can, and as much as we need to, because actually we value it very highly. And as a question of efficiency, because the balance is always to be drawn here between time spent working and time spent learning. And although the more time you spend learning you would be better at working, it takes away from the time you're working. And in a simple equation the income of the firm is determined by the number of hours the lawyers work, not so directly the number of hours they learn. So that balance is quite a difficult one' (Stuart Popham, Senior Partner).
>
> ### Lyreco
>
> 'Two crunches for me I would think would be the amount of time [because] I've got productivity targets to hit. I want to train people and I can't train at the cost of productivity, and I can't drive productivity at the cost of training' (Alistair Wood, Logistics Director).
>
> ### National Audit Office
>
> 'But ... the staff time that goes into it both the time [involved in] being trained, and the time that goes into doing the training. I'm sure I would come up with quite a lot ... so obviously ... that has to be taken into account in our planning' (Tim Burr, Deputy Comptroller and Auditor General).
>
> ### VT plc
>
> '[Learning] is pretty much ingrained in VT culture, but you'll always get quite a few people who nod their heads but don't do it, so a lot of our MDs will revert to the old way of just concentrating on the real today business issue and won't take the time out to invest time, because this does take time. It's surprising actually the amount of money we spend; if we added it all up, on training, learning, investment in people, in pound notes, you know, it's probably in the millions, but it's taking the time out' (Paul Lester, CEO).

that the investment will make a difference to measures that are significant and relevant for their function – not just the agenda and priorities set by LTD.

The size of the organisation will influence perceptions of the nature of the learning investment. Those interviewed from larger organisations tended to discuss their investment in learning processes and activities. By contrast, the salary and overhead investment required just to have a learning function or specialist in place was a significant feature in smaller organisations. Simon Johnson, Director of Corporate Affairs for The Football Association, for example, commented:

I would say our investment is the appointment of a dedicated person, the strengthening of our HR team so that person operates within a strong team that's focused and learning therefore plays its part in the overall employee relations, human resource function.

LEARNING INVESTMENT PROCESSES: ARE THEY ALIGNED?

The interviews highlighted three different but interrelated opportunities for alignment:

- involvement of LTD in business planning process
- proactive development of a value or business case
- management of infrastructure LTD investment.

Each will now be considered in turn.

Business planning process

LTD executives and senior managers in many of the organisations who were interviewed were very aware of the need to ensure that LTD investment decisions were part of regular business planning and budgeting processes in their organisations, as the quotations in Table 2 illustrate.

Effective alignment, then, involves LTD practitioners in formal co-ordination processes. This point is further confirmed by CIPD survey evidence. Data from the CIPD Learning and Development survey, gathered in 2006, indicated that organisations with regular and formalised processes to deliver and review learning and development activities are also more likely to have business-driven learning and development strategies (CIPD 2007a).

VALUE OF LEARNING

Table 2 ◆ Senior managers' and LTD executives' views on LTD investment decisions

	Senior Manager	LTD Executive
Canon UK and Ireland	'We put together an HR business plan for each function at the beginning of a year and that will contain both actions towards a general overall support of our people but also there will be financial implications obviously in costs etc. Some of those costs may well be around internal programmes, some will be around external and some will be skills based. It may be that some of our learning requires additional products or support training. It may require some specific sales or marketing function-based training' (Matthew Norton, Channel Director).	'We have a three-year rolling mid-term plan for our business. ... Every function of our business has this, so there's a growth and productivity element of this, and then there's innovation, there's customer relationships, so all the different elements that you'd probably expect to be in this broader plan. From a learning and development perspective this is specifically captured in the HR plan which cascades from this' (Caroline Price, Strategic Business Partner, HR).
Lyreco	'So in terms of investment from the training side ... we would regularly hold a meeting. ... We discuss...a budget for training, in what form we would require [the training] or what we would want for the next year' (Alistair Wood, Logistics Director).	'[Learning investment] is ...driven through the business planning process and then the actual budget process. So we have our aspirations, hopes and dreams in the business planning that we hope to do with our teams next year. We know what the big picture is from the five year plan of where we should be and we then kind of budget for that' (Ian Lawson, Training and Development Director).

BOX 11: INVESTING IN AND BUDGETING FOR LEARNING

Christian Aid

'Within the organisation, looking at financial investment, at the moment we've got a mish-mash of centralised and de-centralised budgeting. With regard to financial resource allocation towards learning needs, I hold the bulk of that resource' (Jimmy Naudi, Head of Learning and Development).

Clifford Chance

'But the caveat I was going to mention is that my approach is largely to get buy-in from people who are going to champion this kind of thing. That is acknowledging that there are always going to be some people in a firm like this who think general skills training is a waste of time. But I don't think it's the best use of my time trying to convert them. So I am inevitably getting, you know, a more positive response than if I saw a completely random selection' (Julia Clarke, Global Learning and Development Partner).

Dublin City Council

'So HR have an HR budget, and they have a certain capacity for that, and I have my budget and out of that I can make my own judgements. Typically we're pretty positive and supportive of learning' (Kathy Quinn, Head of Finance).

Canon UK and Ireland

'Management leadership training is dealt with through our HR department and our skills and product training is dealt with by our marketing department. So we tend to have two different plans, two different investment processes, although they do come together in the HR plan and they do work together very closely' (Matthew Norton, Channel Director).

VT plc

'But each of the business units has their own budget and the more that I can help the HR directors to be influential and persuasive, the more investment they will get in time, money and resources to put into their budgets. So it's all about: does HR, does learning, add value?' (Jo Robbins, HR Director).

In addition to formal engagement with business planning processes, the interviews also showed how informal dialogue is a vital feature of the learning investment process.

A value or business case

Many of the LTD executives who were interviewed reflected that the ongoing learning investment process involves them in making a case for additional investment, where it is required as a result of emergent business priorities. This influencing process may be formal or informal. Jo Robbins, HR Director for VT plc, for example, commented that throughout the year: 'I have to be influencing the CEO, influencing the other Group Executive Committee members, confronting any negativity I hear – I am straight there, you know. And persuading.'

Whether the influencing processes take place through formal meetings or on an informal basis, the senior management interviewees highlighted the imperative of a business or 'value-case' if learning investments are to be made, as the quotations in Box 12 illustrate.

Management of infrastructure investment

Involvement in business planning processes and the development of a value case to support investment in learning was highlighted by many interviewees. However this was not universally the case. Some interviewees indicated that their organisation operated through a stable pattern of year-on-year 'inherited' training budgets. In such cases LTD practitioners were not necessarily fully involved in the immediate business planning process and a specific 'value-case' was not always required to ensure continued investment.

At first glance this suggests that a passive approach to learning investment decisions may be in place. The consequent danger is that learning processes could 'drift' so that they no longer link or fit clearly with organisational priorities. However there is an alternative interpretation. In some cases this more passive approach may reflect an organisational commitment to continuous investment in learning to ensure ongoing operational effectiveness and long-term capability development. The quotations in Box 13 illustrate this latter point.

Outcome or process?

Three main features of the investment in learning and the decision processes associated with them emerge from the interviews. The need for LTD involvement in the business planning process; the need to proactively make a 'value case' for additional investment; and the commitment in some organisations to invest significantly in meeting 'infrastructure' learning needs. Data from the US study (see Appendix A) highlight similar features whereby 'business unit requirements', 'business priority allocation' and 'enterprise requirements' form the basis upon

---

BOX 12: MAKING THE VALUE-CASE FOR LEARNING INVESTMENT

Canon UK and Ireland

'We had some funding … we put through a group of our account managers and it was a quite expensive course and we ran a couple of courses and it was very successful, very popular, a lot of value to it. We wanted to stick some extra people through it but we didn't have the money. We'd exhausted all the areas of money, so … I decided that I'd pay for that myself. … So we allocated some additional resource. Those are always part of the trade-offs that you have to have in any organisations; the decision as to whether or not to undertake a piece of learning and development because the budgets are tight or whether you do it anyway and overspend. Those are the decisions that do happen as the year progresses' (Matthew Norton, Channel Director).

Clifford Chance

'A good case for additional education and learning will always be backed' (Stuart Popham, Senior Partner).

Schaeffler

'Everything that we have put into the training and learning and change programme we have funded ourselves. … Such was our belief in what we are capable of doing. We had quite an extensive training plan coming out of this, but again we believed that this was a good solid investment that would pay off in the long run' (Roger Evans, Plant Director).

Tesco.com

'But in general, yes we would very rarely embark on something where we couldn't see, build some kind of connection, even if it was quite theoretical, to be able to build a business case' (Laura Wade-Gery, Chief Executive Officer).

BOX 13: INVESTMENT IN INFRASTRUCTURE LTD

Clifford Chance

'Quite a big investment was appointing a partner to lead [learning and development] which hadn't been in place before. ... In terms of financial investment, there hasn't so far been any strategic decision that there is a certain amount of money that we need to spend. It has been more the other way round. I know we need ... to be an employer of choice if you like, so therefore ... we need to be giving top-quality training. ... We need to be doing it so that our people are good at what we are doing. And so it's more looking at that we have the right training to achieve that and then we see how much that costs' (Julia Clarke, Global Learning and Development Partner).

National Audit Office

'We don't have an annual business planning process where we review what we spend, what we budget, where of course everything is totted up, and the inevitable trade-offs are made. That, thus far, has only really [made] a marginal effect on the investment that we make in our programmes. I should add that we make a significant investment in our graduate training. We train around 70 chartered accountants a year and that is very different from the position that we were in certainly 20 years ago, 15 years ago, 10 years ago. So the last five years we've doubled the numbers of people and again that's based on an assessment that we have to invest that money to maintain a professional workforce that can deliver a credible quality product' (Julian Wood, Director of Development and Employment).

---

which learning investment decisions are made in US organisations (Sugrue et al 2006).

In the interviews relating to alignment, the issues raised reveal some interesting features of practical relevance to senior managers and learning decision-makers.

First, proactive activity by LTD practitioners, both as a formal part of regular business planning processes and also through informal dialogue with other stakeholders, is very important. This is because budgets with implications for learning may be dispersed throughout the organisation and may be the responsibility of a range of different managers. Further, achieving financial investment is only part of the issue, as LTD practitioners also need to be able to persuade managers to invest in time to enable learning to take place so that the benefits of the financial investment can be realised.

Second, the involvement of LTD practitioners in regular business planning processes is vital to enable alignment of investment in learning with organisational priorities. In addition, however, LTD practitioners have to be able to influence decision-makers and budget holders, both formally and informally, to invest in additional learning priorities that may emerge outside the formal business planning process. In such situations managers are unlikely to agree to further investment without a supporting value or business case.

Third, for some organisations a large proportion of learning investment may be inherited year-on-year with the expectation that it will be directed to ongoing and established training and development processes. In such cases it is important that LTD practitioners guard against a 'drift' of learning and development processes away from emerging organisational priorities. Where such a pattern of investment is a strategic necessity, it is particularly important that LTD practitioners ensure a cost-effective use of this investment.

The Clifford Chance case illustration (below) provides an example of one organisation where investment in high levels of ongoing training and education as well as in shorter-term business imperatives is required.

CASE ILLUSTRATION

Clifford Chance

Clifford Chance is one of the world's largest law firms, operating through 27 offices in 20 countries. Over 3,800 highly qualified professionals are employed worldwide. Learning is a key issue for the competitive success of this high-quality, professional services organisation. In early 2007, in recognition of the important contribution learning and development makes to organisational effectiveness, the firm appointed a Global Learning and Development Partner to ensure alignment between learning and the needs of the business.

Lawyers working in busy law firms, who earn their fees by the hour, find it difficult to make time for learning. Thus, a key challenge for the organisation is to build a learning and development culture so that partners and employees will invest the time that is needed for appropriate development.

In order to maintain and develop its position as a leading global law firm, Clifford Chance has to invest in significant year-on-year training, continuous development and education for employees and partners. However, in addition Julia Clarke, the Global Learning and Development Partner, is convinced that her role requires agreeing and integrating learning and development to meet the strategic priorities of the firm and she comments

> that her role involves 'making sure we are close to the business and so ensuring that the learning and development function is aligned with the business'.
>
> For Clifford Chance, therefore, alignment involves ensuring that 'infrastructure' training and development is delivered in a cost-effective way. It also involves identifying and delivering strategic interventions in managing knowledge, information and learning, to enable the organisation to achieve its aspiration of becoming the world's premier law firm offering consistently high standards of client service across the full range of business legal practice areas.

MEASURING ONGOING ALIGNMENT

Aligning initial learning investment processes with business priorities is clearly a central issue. The dynamic nature of alignment processes means that LTD practitioners must be aware of the danger of 'drift' away from organisational priorities. The maintenance and measurement of ongoing alignment is, therefore, particularly important and this was addressed by the fourth question asked in the semi-structured interviews which was:

> How do you know the learning function is maintaining ongoing alignment with your organisation's strategic business needs?

Responses to this question were characterised by a lack of reference, even by LTD executives, to the use of traditional learning needs analysis or training planning and monitoring processes to ensure ongoing alignment. Also, almost one-third of the senior managers who participated in this study indicated that they did not really know how the learning function ensured it maintained ongoing alignment. This had also been found to be the case in the US study (Sugrue et al 2006), where researchers found evidence of what they termed 'misalignment' in almost a third of responses. In the CIPD study interviewees highlighted two main ways through which their organisations monitor the ongoing alignment of learning with organisational priorities. These are:

- dialogue between LTD and line-managers
- use of internal or external measures or metrics.

Each approach will now be considered in turn.

Maintaining alignment through dialogue

The research highlights that fact that continuous dialogue between LTD practitioners and line managers is a vital part of maintaining ongoing alignment. Three particular avenues of dialogue were indicated:

- the opportunity to participate in regular business progress meetings with line management colleagues.
- participation in forums with a range of stakeholders to discuss learning and its role and contribution in the organisation
- the development of informal working relationships with line managers – taking their needs as internal customers seriously and ensuring their involvement in monitoring learning processes.

The quotations in Box 14 illustrate these themes.

The need for effective working relationships with other stakeholders was also a clear theme in many of the responses to the Value of Learning online discussion thread (see Appendix A). Here contributors emphasised the necessity of integrating LTD objectives and plans with business goals and for an ongoing dialogue to ensure continuing alignment. The three extracts from the discussion thread in Box 15 illustrate this point.

An important way for organisations to ensure that learning achieves ongoing alignment with organisational priorities, therefore, is through dialogue between LTD and line managers. Sometimes this is conducted formally and involves discussion of business progress. However a significant part of dialogue with managers may also be informal. A contributor to the CIPD value of learning discussion thread, for example, pointed out:

> *The challenge is that managers still do not see learning and development as a strategic resource which can help them achieve their business objectives (Bola Owoade, contributor to the online discussion thread on 21 November 2006).*

Organisational measures of alignment

A key challenge for LTD practitioners, therefore, is to make a persuasive case for the value of learning for the organisation. One way this can be achieved is through the use of measures and metrics.

These were highlighted by more than half of the organisations as a further way by which they ensured the ongoing organisational alignment of learning. Reflections or comments about the use of internal or external measures and metrics to assess ongoing alignment came from public, private and not-for profit sector organisations. In fact the senior operational managers reflected on the use of measures to assess ongoing alignment more than LTD executives did. Some highlighted the use of external benchmarks to assess ongoing alignment, while others stressed the use of internal organisational metrics and measures to make this assessment.

Four organisations highlighted the use of external benchmarks: two were public sector, one was a not-for-profit organisation and the other was a private sector company. In reflecting on the use of benchmarks, interviewees indicated that they were reassured of ongoing alignment if, through benchmarking, the learning function for their organisation could demonstrate that it was operating in accordance with 'best practice'.

The use of internal key performance indicators and metrics was

> ### BOX 14: THE IMPORTANCE OF DIALOGUE WITH ORGANISATION STAKEHOLDERS
>
> #### Canon UK and Ireland
>
> 'We have a very close alignment. Each of the people who do my job have senior managers of HR that they spend a lot of time with and [they also spend time with] the senior managers in the group. [The HR Director] spends a lot of time discussing those issues and the HR function has a major part to play in all of our weekly senior management meetings or our monthly offsite meetings, so it would be difficult for them to escape' (Matthew Norton, Channel Director).
>
> #### Dublin City Council
>
> 'I think the other pieces that ensure ... alignment are the Corporate Partnership Forum Training and Development Network that meets quarterly. All change and modernisation [processes] agreed for the organisation go through that process so they are very aware of what's happening within the organisation. It's another check if you like in terms of the checks and balances for me, that the training plan fits with that modernisation agenda and progresses it' (Maire Twomey, Training Manager).
>
> #### The Football Association
>
> 'How do we keep up with that? Well, I guess it's a mixture of best practice, what's going to work well, knowing that the management team know that we need to change. They're articulating that change through a strategy. We need to build a relationship with them so that we are involved in helping to deliver that strategy' (Tom Harlow, Learning and Development Manager).
>
> #### Lyreco
>
> 'But I think that if you have that healthy respect for [managers] as customers in the first place then it gives you a different kind of relationship. You have to bite your tongue sometimes because it's that old adage that ... the customer might not always be right but then they always are the customer. So it's about making sure that the level of support they are getting from people in my team is actually right and correct at that moment in time' (Ian Lawson, Training and Development Director).
>
> #### Schaeffler
>
> 'It's a review process, a review strategy – is it still right for us? We always ask that question whenever we go back and look at the strategy: Are we doing the right thing? Is it having the right effect? Should we carry on with this? Should we drop that one? Do we do more of this and less of that one? Which has the most effect? It's not always easy to determine that because time is involved and you have to give these things more time. It's in the review process and the results, of course; if you can tie some of the results back to some of these softer issues then it gives us some indication of whether we are doing the right thing and doing it well' (Roger Evans, Plant Director).

highlighted by interviewees from five other organisations (all but one of which were private sector companies). Measures that were particularly prominent included: customer satisfaction measures, productivity measures, management succession indicators and employee retention.

CONCLUSION

This chapter has underlined the importance of alignment for a strategic approach to LTD. Such an approach provides LTD practitioners with a way of articulating how learning can contribute to competitive advantage. Such an approach gives direction to learning.

Feedback from the interviews indicates that some organisations measure ongoing alignment through key performance indicators. Others measure alignment through comparison with external benchmark standards. External benchmark measures are most likely to be used in situations where most of an organisation's learning investment is directed at maintaining ongoing, year-on-year training and education processes. For organisations where investment in learning is more closely linked to a fit with immediate or short-term business priorities, internal metrics to assess the extent of ongoing alignment are more likely. This is illustrated in Figure 5.

Achieving alignment presents a number of challenges. Learning investment processes in most organisations may easily become fragmented as learning activities are often funded through a variety of different budgets that are the responsibility of a range of organisational stakeholders. In addition, achieving an investment in time needed for learning can be just as important as agreeing a financial investment. In some organisations a significant part of the investment in learning is devoted to

BOX 15: DIALOGUE – SOME PRACTITIONER PERSPECTIVES

'There is a very open two-way communication in our organisation and feedback is always given by senior management about training effectiveness. This provides valuable input for our L&D strategy. I think there is more awareness of the value of learning, as although there are budget limitations, once a proposal is put forward to the senior team and they buy into the benefits, then it is rarely discounted for cost reasons. L&D priorities are identified through metrics such as voice of the customer – guest satisfaction data, key priorities for the business in the coming year based on key performance indicators, and employee engagement data. Additionally monthly meetings are held between the L&D Manager and departmental trainers (based in the operational departments) to ensure alignment of training focus with organisational strategy' (Anne Zammit Lupi, contributor to the online discussion thread on 23 November 2006).

'As a Learning and Development manager, I saw one of the most important parts of my role was that of championing our products with our internal customers. This view started with finding out managers' learning needs, those of their staff and discussing with them the best ways that we might help them meet their objectives. The programmes we designed we checked out with a number of managers during the design and piloting stages of any intervention, making amendments according to their feedback. This was an important part of validating the usefulness of what we offered.

'The other important part of the dialogue was the word of mouth reputation of the L&D team. We found that individual learners accessed them or our intranet to discuss their needs and issues. HR advisers referred others to us, and past satisfied customers also passed the word around. I'm not sure how you measure this, but we had a rough appreciation of the areas of the business where our enquiries came from, and a plan to access those parts we had as yet failed to reach – and put a rough percentage on this each year to judge progress in our influence and perceived value. My impression was that they found us a valuable resource in helping them sort out their issues (consultancy), deal with individual issues (coaching), and as a resource to design and deliver helpful group interventions (programmes, team development etc) which each had different objectives.

'Interestingly, the more the dialogue grew, the less important doing formal evaluation seemed to be, we hoped that this was seen as an indication that we were doing a professional job' (Jennifer Taylor, contributor to the online discussion thread on 18 December 2006).

'For me, the process starts with meeting business managers, going to their meetings and asking questions. The more interested we are, the more we talk with them, the more we understand the business and the issues, the more we get invited to their meetings, their social events, their presentations, the more we learn about what their business needs. From those conversations, come the learning needs. I would then check my understanding of those learning needs with the business managers. I would ask something like "what can you do in your role as their manager and coach to help people learn what you say they need?" All this is before any discussion about training plans or classroom solutions' (Hugh Spalding, contributor to the online discussion thread on 2 January 2007).

ongoing 'year-on-year' training and development processes and in such cases the focus is on the cost-effective use of resources.

For most organisations the principal way of ensuring that learning investment is aligned with organisational priorities is through the involvement of LTD practitioners in the business planning process. Proactive activity by LTD practitioners outside of regular business planning processes and based on a business or a 'value-case' is necessary where specific learning needs are identified outside of the business planning process.

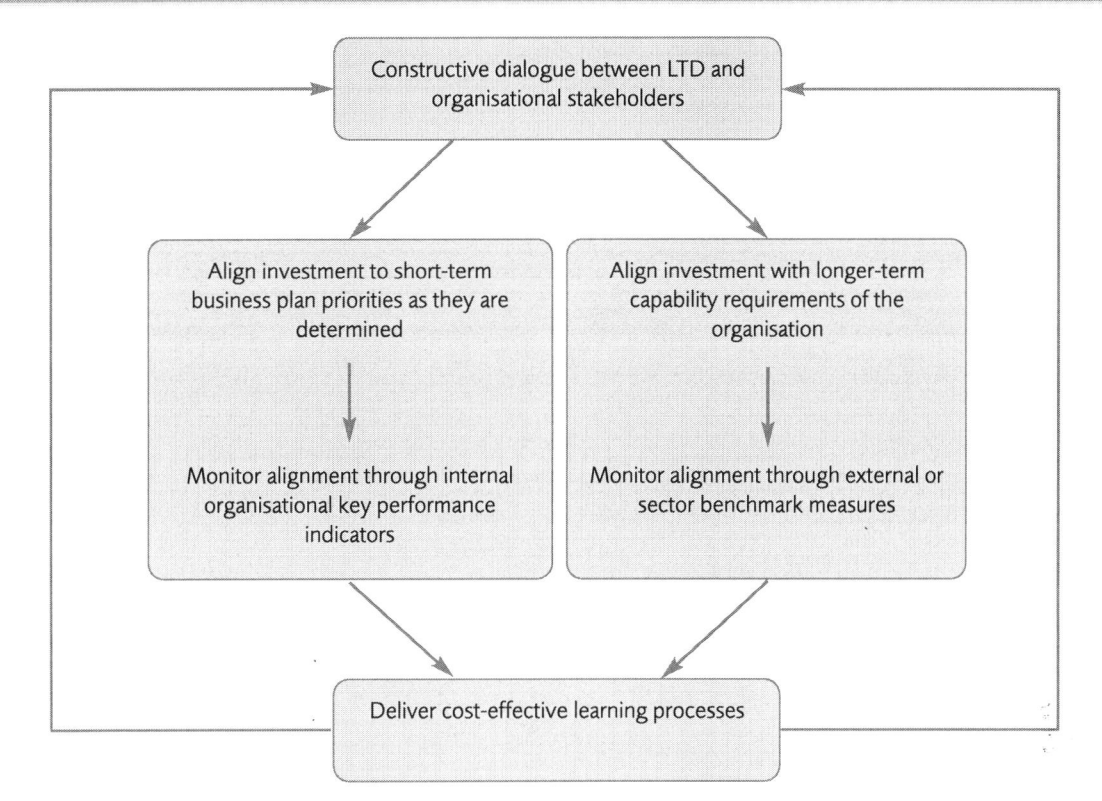

Figure 5 The alignment process

```
                    ┌─────────────────────────────────────┐
          ┌────────▶│ Constructive dialogue between LTD and│◀────────┐
          │         │     organisational stakeholders      │         │
          │         └─────────────────────────────────────┘         │
          │              │                        │                   │
          │              ▼                        ▼                   │
          │  ┌──────────────────────┐  ┌──────────────────────┐      │
          │  │ Align investment to  │  │ Align investment with│      │
          │  │ short-term business  │  │ longer-term          │      │
          │  │ plan priorities as   │  │ capability           │      │
          │  │ they are determined  │  │ requirements of the  │      │
          │  │                      │  │ organisation         │      │
          │  └──────────────────────┘  └──────────────────────┘      │
          │              │                        │                   │
          │              ▼                        ▼                   │
          │  ┌──────────────────────┐  ┌──────────────────────┐      │
          │  │ Monitor alignment    │  │ Monitor alignment    │      │
          │  │ through internal     │  │ through external or  │      │
          │  │ organisational key   │  │ sector benchmark     │      │
          │  │ performance          │  │ measures             │      │
          │  │ indicators           │  │                      │      │
          │  └──────────────────────┘  └──────────────────────┘      │
          │              │                        │                   │
          │              ▼                        ▼                   │
          │         ┌─────────────────────────────────────┐          │
          └─────────│ Deliver cost-effective learning processes │──────┘
                    └─────────────────────────────────────┘
```

MEASURING AND REPORTING 5

- **Senior managers welcome qualitative as well as quantitative assessments of the value of learning.**

- **Four main approaches to measuring and reporting on value can be identified: learning function efficiency measures, key performance indicators and benchmark measures, return on investment measures, and return on expectation measures.**

- **Performance against key performance indicators and benchmarks is a frequently used approach taken to measure the value of learning.**

- **Organisations are moving away from return on investment approaches, preferring to develop return on expectation measures.**

INTRODUCTION

This chapter considers how organisations are meeting the challenges of measuring the strategic value of LTD outcomes and processes. It reviews feedback from the final three questions asked in the semi-structured interviews:

- How do you measure the learning function's value contribution to your organisation today?

- How do you know that the learning function is functioning as efficiently as possible?

- What information is used for measuring and reporting on value?

Achieving a strategic approach to people development requires evaluation methods and reasoning processes that reflect the concerns of key stakeholders in an organisation. Importantly different organisational stakeholders have different perceptions of the value of learning and different expectations of the organisational contribution that they expect from LTD. As indicated in Chapter 3, senior decision-makers expect learning to ensure the strategic readiness of employees, deliver performance improvement and cost-effective labour, and enable effective career or talent-management processes. In addition, stakeholders in the organisation expect to be reassured that the LTD function is operating in a cost-effective and efficient way in achieving this value contribution.

Traditional evaluation methods, which focus on the experiences of learners and trainers, can offer some information about the efficiency and effectiveness of learning operations but they do not address the wider organisational expectations of the learning value contribution. Therefore, this chapter explores how decision-makers in organisations are developing measures and reporting on the contribution of learning at this wider organisational level.

Three interrelated questions are considered. First, what measures are being used to assess the LTD value contribution to the organisation as a whole? Second, what measures are used to assess whether the LTD function is operating as efficiently as possible? Third, what are the key challenges that organisations face as they develop their approaches to measurement and reporting on the value of learning?

Each will be considered in turn.

ASSESSING THE LEARNING VALUE CONTRIBUTION

The fifth question asked in the face-to-face interviews was:

> How do you measure the learning function's value contribution to your organisation today?

This proved to be a challenging question for the participants in the Value of Learning project. Interviewees from almost every organisation indicated that this issue was still 'work in progress' rather than something that they had already established. The quotations from the interviews in Box 16 illustrate the main points that were made.

The interviewees also indicated that quantitative data alone does not adequately reflect the intangible value that learning processes can generate as the quotations in Box 17 illustrate.

The complex and emergent nature of many learning outcomes therefore, is accepted by many senior managers. Effective dialogue with LTD, in addition to hard data, contributes to senior management perceptions that learning is adding value to the organisation as a whole.

BOX 16: DEVELOPING MEASURES AS 'WORK IN PROGRESS'

Glasgow Housing Association

'This is one of the challenges for us. We are at an early stage of working with managers to get them to measure the business benefits of learning undertaken, this is being incorporated as part of our personal development planning process' (Anne Fitzsimmons, Learning and Development Manager).

The Innovation Group

'Well, right now it's very difficult for us to measure because we don't have too many metrics in place' (Shaun Gwilliam, Software Solutions Director).

VT Group plc

'We haven't developed good enough KPIs yet. I think it's just from my own personal point of view, when I go round and visit companies, which we do a lot, it's just talking, getting people to talk about what they're doing; any issues they've got, and it is people's attitude' (Paul Lester, CEO).

The Football Association

'I view this as the kind of thing that, after a year of operation, you turn round and we should be told, "Here's the function and now here's how we're going to measure it," and then we'll make an assessment of it' (Simon Johnson, Director of Corporate Affairs, The Football Association).

BOX 17: MEASURING COMPLEXITY

The Football Association

'I can feel that there's an intangible benefit that I can see now. … I think people just feel better about the options that are available to them, they feel empowered to improve themselves, and they feel that the company are helping them to do it. And if I, as a manager, give that impression, that open impression … then that's all positive' (Simon Johnson, Director of Corporate Affairs).

Lyreco

'Once again, it's very hard to measure other than all the people involved were motivated after [a particular learning] event and all the people that were involved had a real buzz factor from it. All I know is that they did make a difference and they felt good about themselves and about Lyreco for being involved in the project. So it's hard to measure in cash terms, but in terms of development and feel-good factor, its right up there' (Ian Lawson, Training and Development Director).

Dublin City Council

'We don't have an explicit measure, no. And maybe that's because it's kind of dispersed between the bulk of the team in the things that you're doing. They're each taking action on that, getting on with it' (Kathy Quinn, Head of Finance).

A number of different categories of measures were highlighted in the interviews as ways of assessing the learning function's value contribution. The following main groupings emerged and are considered in turn:

- learning function efficiency measures
- key performance indicators and benchmark measures
- return on investment
- return on expectation.

Learning function efficiency measures

For senior managers, internal benchmark and KPI indicators were particularly important in determining the contribution of learning to the organisation. However LTD executives focused more on the learning function efficiency measures in their responses and these are considered first.

Traditional evaluation measures that focus on the efficiency and effectiveness of learning processes and interventions were cited by half of the LTD interviewees as ways of measuring the contribution of learning. Learner feedback data and 'happy sheets' were most frequently mentioned and other pre-learning and post-programme data, collected by the LTD function, were also highlighted as being ways of assessing the value contribution. Examples of these sorts of 'learning function' measures are presented in Appendix C.

Such information is useful to LTD practitioners and addresses important questions such as:

- Is the LTD function delivering operational effectiveness?
- How effectively is the functional capability of the workforce being developed?
- How well are learning interventions supporting critical success factors?
- How do learning operations compare with those of other relevant organisations?

However, although these sorts of measures are useful to LTD practitioners none of the senior managers cited these as indicators of the learning function's value contribution. This adds weight to the view that traditional evaluation data has limited relevance for non-LTD stakeholders in the organisation.

Key performance indicators and benchmark measures

As indicated in Chapter 3 (page 16) regular measurement to indicate performance against organisational targets, KPIs or benchmarks was frequently highlighted in the semi-structured interviews. This was seen as a way of assessing the overall contribution of learning to the organisation. Almost all of the senior management interviewees discussed the use of information related to internal targets or key performance indicators, and in half of these cases their views were also shared by the LTD executive for that organisation. Appendix C provides indicative examples of measures that can be used. Those that were cited most in the interviews included:

- staff satisfaction
- customer satisfaction
- productivity
- management succession indicators
- service quality delivery
- sales targets and sales margins
- employee retention.

Staff satisfaction measures were highlighted particularly by the LTD interviewees, whereas senior managers also indicated the importance of other data, for example customer satisfaction and recruitment and retention benchmarks.

The quotations in Table 3 illustrate some of the main points raised in response to this question.

Achievements against benchmark or key performance indicators are important measures of the value of learning, therefore. This finding was also a feature of the US study into the value of learning where 'organisational outcomes' such as business results, employee satisfaction, customer satisfaction and turnover were features of the approaches cited as measures of the value of learning (Sugrue et al 2006).

In both the UK and the USA, therefore, this approach to assessing the value of learning addresses important questions such as:

- To what extent are business process efficiency targets and objectives being met?
- How does organisational performance compare with that of other relevant organisations?
- Are employees developing in line with the emerging needs of the business?
- To what extent is an appropriate psychological contract with employees being developed?

Return on investment (ROI)

One of the most interesting features which emerged from the semi-structured interviews undertaken in the UK was the evident shift that is occurring from return on investment (ROI) measures towards a focus on return on expectation (ROE) measures.

ROI approaches involve calculating the 'bottom line' impact of training or learning interventions. This sort of economic 'proof' of the value of learning is an attractive proposition for those who work in LTD. Indeed responses to the second online poll were overwhelmingly positive to the proposition that: 'Statistical

MEASURING AND REPORTING

Table 3 ❖ Senior managers' and LTD executives' views on benchmark measures

	Senior manager	LTD Executive
National Audit Office	'A comprehensive staff survey ... which gave us a pretty good picture of what people think of their managers and how satisfied they are with the way the organisation works. ... But I think above and beyond that, it's partly a question of the sort of feel of the organisation' (Tim Burr, Deputy Comptroller and Auditor General).	'We also now run a staff survey. ... This year we've done a staff survey and we've included all the questions from the old Good People Managers survey and were delighted to find that the results were substantially better than they were three or four years ago when we last ran the staff survey' (Julian Wood, Director of Development and Employment).
Tesco.com	'What I'm looking for is consistent improvement in that steering wheel [balanced scorecard] year on year. Continuing improvement year on year' (Laura Wade-Gery, CEO).	'What is really important is that Tesco hit the targets on this - it affects the bonus. So each area and quadrant of the steering wheel [balanced scorecard] will have measures and targets and then you'll make that work in your own function. ... Unless we hit green across these five areas of the steering wheel, the bonus is affected' (Therese Procter, Personnel Director).
VT plc	'We do customer surveys ... but we could do with more. And, of course, customer feedback. If you've got employee feedback and customer feedback you've got a pretty good picture of what's going on in the business' (Paul Lester, CEO).	'We ... do it through questionnaires, in the main, because we have about 13,000 employees, which is quite high, so it is really the only way of getting at the grass roots' (Jo Robbins, HR Director).

measures should be used to establish the return on investment (ROI) of learning activities' (see Appendix B).

The Value of Learning interviews provided the opportunity to probe this further and suggested that the picture is more complex. The aim of ROI is to verify the amount of return that has been achieved through defining the outcomes of the training or learning intervention and determining how much it has cost. Whilst ROI measures set out to provide an economic indicator of the value of training to the 'bottom line', this presents a number of difficulties. First, the calculation of an ROI assessment requires that the training is already completed and the costs known. This therefore presents problems of timeliness, and traditional ROI metrics and measures do not take future benefits into consideration. A second difficult area is the quantification of consequences of learning that are intangible, even though they are explicit. Another difficulty is the interrelated nature of many processes and variables that underpin organisational performance and value creation such that it is not reasonable or possible to identify simple cause and effect variables attributable to learning.

ROI approaches to evaluation, therefore, address organisational questions such as:

❖ What economic benefits are directly attributable to learning interventions?

❖ How is the contribution made by learning directly affecting the achievement of HR targets?

❖ How cost-effective are learning and training interventions?

❖ How is training contributing directly to the achievement of performance targets?

When discussing measures of the learning function's value contribution, only three organisations mentioned any form of ROI measure. Further, senior management interviewees were less concerned than their LTD colleagues about ROI measures. Those who did reflect on ROI highlighted its specific use following interventions such as sales and account management courses and management of absence courses.

This suggests that ROI approaches are only appropriate when the costs of the intervention can be calculated in a straightforward way, the goals of the intervention are clearly specified and relate to defined performance targets, and the impact of the training can be assessed over a defined period of time.

Return on expectation (ROE)

In place of ROI approaches, however, interviewees described the development of what can be termed return on expectation (ROE) measures of the value of learning. This involves focusing on establishing 'up front' the anticipated benefits of learning interventions or investments with key stakeholders, and then assessing the extent to which the anticipated benefits have been realised. In addition to 'hard' numerical information interviewees also highlighted the scope for 'softer' more qualitative data to assess ROE.

More than half of the organisations offered examples of this ROE approach. Some illustrations are given in Box 18.

The semi-structured interviews suggested that using ROI as the 'bottom line' may not be the best criteria for determining the value of learning. For a small range of learning interventions it may be a good indicator but it is not *the* indicator. Instead the interviews pointed to the usefulness of ROE measures as part of the assessment of the value of learning.

Such ROE measures, examples of which are provided in Appendix C, take into account qualitative 'soft' assessments as well as quantitative numerical measures. They assess changes that have occurred as a result of learning processes and the extent to which stakeholder expectations have been met. This emergent approach to value and evaluation, therefore, addresses questions such as:

- To what extent are employees learning to exhibit the behavioural competences that are required?

- How successfully are management succession and talent pool issues being managed?

- To what extent do the organisation's people skills support the mitigation of risks to achieving strategic objectives?

- To what extent are organisational learning and growth targets being met?

Some of the LTD practitioner contributors to the online discussion thread that formed part of the Value of Learning project (see Appendix A) also took the opportunity of reflecting on the opportunities and issues presented by a move from ROI to ROE. Two further points about ROE emerged from the discussion thread.

BOX 18: RETURN ON EXPECTATION MEASURES

Canon UK and Ireland

'We do some pre-course analysis on the individual, on their current scenario, and we contract with their line manager ... and then post-programme they have a project which is linked to the programme where they have to either create a cost reduction or create an added value to our business of a set amount ... that otherwise they wouldn't have done had they not gone onto that programme. It's very focused in trying to cement some hard, tangible return' (Caroline Price, Strategic Business Partner, HR).

'We did a contracted coaching relationship with them up front: "this is what we will and won't cover and how we're going to measure it." We did some 360 degree feedback for most of them at the end of that period ... but there was also anecdotal evidence around the business' (Caroline Price, Strategic Business Partner, HR).

Glasgow Housing Association

'It's ... about making sure that what we are delivering for managers and teams is actually meeting their needs. And it is not having to go back and keep repeating the same learning intervention' (Anne Fitzsimmons, Learning and Development Manager).

Lyreco

'What we have tried to do is make sure that [we] understand where a department or a person started from and what is the pain, what is the issue for that team or department? And then ... [develop] some kind of learning intervention [that] can help. ... And if we know clearly when we are going into something where people are, then we can measure what we have managed to do' (Ian Lawson, Training and Development Director).

Schaeffler

'As you know, "using figures and financial results is like driving by looking in the rear view mirror!" ... We like to think we are so much in tune with what's going on that the scorecard is actually just a confirmation of what we know already in lots of ways. We have an understanding of what is going on ... and that comes back to the questions ... yes – you need to ask the right questions to ensure that you get that right approach' (Roger Evans, Plant Director).

VT plc

'So each programme that we do ... has good measurements mapped out nice and clearly. The main thing, of course, is how well we are doing. ... We are still working on the action plans for that. ... It is quite interesting in that we tried to do qualitative rather than quantitative. ... We wanted to make it more fun, really interesting and also more insightful than a tick-box exercise. So we did focus groups and we had them drawing pictures of VT on a good day, VT on bad day, VT as an object. We are still working them out at the moment and we will continue with the employee questionnaires' (Jo Robbins, HR Director).

First, the importance of being alert to the possibility that stakeholder expectations about what learning can deliver may change over time. Second, the importance for LTD professionals of contributing to and influencing expectations about the contribution that learning can make. The extracts from the CIPD value of learning discussion thread in Box 19 illustrate these points.

These quotations illustrate how a move from ROI to an ROE approach involves LTD practitioners in finding out and influencing the original expectations of organisational stakeholders. In addition, through dialogue, LTD practitioners must monitor the extent to which those expectations change over time and must work to maintain commitment levels to agreed learning processes. An ROE approach may also require LTD practitioners to engage constructively with stakeholders to identify priorities and develop realistic expectations. The shift from ROI towards more of an ROE approach in practice is illustrated in the following organisational example.

CASE ILLUSTRATION

Canon UK and Ireland

Canon UK forms a major part of the European operation of Canon Inc., the well-known Japanese corporation that specialises in all forms of imaging products. The organisation delivers leading-edge imaging technologies to both domestic and business customers. The potential to innovate and bring pioneering new developments to market is a key issue for this fast-moving company.

Measuring and reporting on the value of learning is a key issue for Canon UK. One way of assessing the value of learning at Canon is through monitoring key organisational indicators for HR priorities such as recruitment and retention, employee satisfaction and pay. In addition senior decision-makers at Canon are aware that a key contribution of learning is to equip the organisation to meet future-orientated challenges. Therefore it is also important that measures of value are future orientated. 'Return on investment' models for assessing the value of learning are tailored accordingly to focus more on 'return on expectation' and achievement against business targets. In line with this, Canon makes sure that some measures of value are built into the learning design process for major corporate learning initiatives.

A challenge, however, is to ensure that inappropriate data is not 'forced' into a metric for the sake of completeness. Evaluating 'what is different' as a result of learning processes in the organisation is as important as completing a numerical assessment. Numerical and quantifiable data, therefore, are complemented by informal and often anecdotal assessments of the value that learning is adding to the business, and Canon is aware that 'soft' measures can be just as useful as hard data. Like many organisations, therefore, Canon has come some way with the process of assessing and reporting on the value of learning but it is also aware that there is scope for further work in this important area.

The research identifies an important shift in perspective. Feedback from the interviews suggests that organisations are developing four main types of measures of the value of learning. Learning function efficiency measures are one way to assess the value contribution. Such approaches ensure that the LTD function is operating in a cost-effective and efficient way. A second set of measures makes use of performance metrics relating to key performance indicators or benchmarks. The third and fourth can be regarded as 'return on …' measures. As the utility of the traditional return on investment approaches is seen to be limited, so return on expectation measures are being developed. This involves establishing 'up front' the anticipated benefits of learning interventions or investments and then assessing the extent to which the anticipated benefits have been realised.

BOX 19: RETURN ON EXPECTATION – THE PRACTITIONER PERSPECTIVE

'Stakeholders or sponsors might request that development is put in place but to what extent do they take an interest in it once they have passed the request on to others whose task it is to make it happen? Also, to what extent do those responsible for learning and development engage with the sponsor or client – to identify what is really wanted and why? If learning and development is to genuinely deliver value for those who seek it, the value as perceived by the relevant people needs to be well understood, articulated and shared. If what is really valued has not been identified and explored, it will be difficult for learning and development to fully deliver what is needed. Sometimes what is needed or wanted may not always be achievable. Choices may have to be made, priorities identified – and agreed' (Neil Offley, contributor to the online discussion thread on 2 May 2007).

'Learning and development should not be just an order taker. … We should be influencing business leaders' expectations. Many managers may not even understand that they need development or what sort of development should be provided, never mind how it should be evaluated. So even if an organisation employs that rare breed of manager who actually want to see an ROI calculation, learning and development needs to decide whether it should accept or challenge the situation' (Jon Ingham, contributor to the online discussion thread on 7 May 2007).

VALUE OF LEARNING

MEASURING THE EFFICIENCY OF THE LEARNING FUNCTION

The focus of this report will now shift to the sixth question that was asked in the semi-structured interviews:

> How do you know that the learning function is functioning as efficiently as possible?

Again responses to this question highlight that 'work is in progress'. Developing appropriate metrics for learning and development is part of the 'to do' list in many organisations. Indeed, interviewees from eight of the 12 organisations that participated in the project indicated that they would like more explicit measures.

It is interesting that learning function efficiency measures were highlighted by interviewees, particularly by the LTD executives, in response to two questions: Question 5 ('How do you measure the learning function's value contribution to your organisation today?') and Question 6 ('How do you know that the learning function is functioning as efficiently as possible?'). Responses to the latter question provide an opportunity to probe more deeply into this important issue.

Interviewees from more than half of the organisations highlighted the importance of using learning operations data to assess the efficiency of their learning function. Appendix C provides some examples of these measures and, reflecting the variety of organisational priorities and strategies, different indicators were highlighted by interviewees from different organisations. Indicators most frequently mentioned included:

- annual spend on learning and training
- cost of training per participant
- rate of internal promotions
- achievement against learning and growth scorecard targets.

In addition to the learning function efficiency metrics, interviewees, particularly the senior managers, highlighted the importance of less formal and less numerical perceptions. They indicated that qualitative and informal feedback was important to reassure them about the efficiency of the learning function. They also stressed the importance of incorporating intangible perceptions into an assessment of efficiency and effectiveness. The quotations in Box 20 illustrate these points.

The information from the interviews considered in this chapter, therefore, highlights the importance of using qualitative (informal and perceptual) information as well as numerical metrics. This applies both to the assessment of the LTD value contribution to the organisation as a whole and to determining whether the LTD function is operating as efficiently as possible. In addition, the interview data shows how value of learning measures are in the early stages of development in most organisations.

MEASURING AND REPORTING

This 'direction of travel' for value and evaluation was further explored though asking some final questions on the challenges and opportunities presented by the development of metrics and measures. These questions were:

> **Measuring and reporting**
>
> a) Please could you describe any form of benchmarking or 'scorecard' measurement that you undertake here regarding learning and development?
>
> b) What challenges and opportunities do the benchmarking or scorecards approach to measurement provide for you?
>
> c) How meaningful is the benchmarking or scorecard data for senior managers?

The responses confirmed the importance for senior managers of measuring the value of learning. Interviewees were clear about the importance of measures of performance against benchmarks and KPIs such as staff satisfaction, productivity, recruitment and retention, as well as accident or health and safety measures. In addition many described internal scorecard or business plans which featured learning and growth targets as an important business issue. Interviewees from public, private and not-for-profit sector organisations of all sizes highlighted how the use of measures and metrics enable the learning function to communicate in a meaningful way with the rest of the organisation and with senior managers in particular. The quotations in Box 21 illustrate this point.

These quotations illustrate the benefits experienced by interviewees in organisations that were developing measures of the value of learning. However, interviewees were also conscious of some of the challenges involved in this process. Three main areas of challenge were highlighted.

First, both senior managers and LTD executives highlighted the need to ensure the validity and reliability of the measures being used (whether they really provide evidence, in a reliable way, on what they are supposed to be about). Second, LTD executives in particular highlighted the challenges of collecting data where learning processes are decentralised and dispersed throughout different parts of the organisation. Third, both LTD and senior management interviewees acknowledged the difficulty of measuring in a quantitative way the dynamic and multidimensional nature of many learning processes. These points are illustrated in the quotations in Box 22.

CONCLUSION

A strategic approach to people development means that LTD professionals must develop methods of evaluating and assessing the value of learning that reflect the concerns of key stakeholders in the organisation, particularly senior managers. Many organisations are at the beginning of a journey towards the

> ### BOX 20: INFORMAL FEEDBACK ABOUT THE EFFICIENCY OF THE LEARNING FUNCTION
>
> #### Canon UK and Ireland
>
> 'I know because we work with them very closely so it's quite difficult for us to escape each other. We take feedback from individuals who've been on these learning programmes. ... We take an interest in how they're progressing. Also non-learning function people tend to be involved in all learning functional theatres. ... We would be able to know quite quickly whether something is working well, in our opinion, or not well'.
>
> 'I guess one of the gut feeling measures that I use to check whether the learning [function] is working efficiently is, "how willing are they to change and adapt the programmes that they have in place to take account of feedback?"' (Matthew Norton, Channel Director).
>
> #### The Football Association
>
> 'I can intangibly see that there has been an improvement. Lots of people know more about a number of things around the business, not just the business but key developments' (Simon Johnson, Director of Corporate Affairs).
>
> #### Glasgow Housing Association
>
> 'A lot of it comes via "off the cuff" feedback. A lot of it is not formal ... but from one-to-one discussion, meeting with the managers and staff to talk about their priorities and where they see themselves, where we can add value. ... You also find a lot of anecdotal evidence' (Anne Fitzsimmons, Learning and Development Manager).
>
> #### Schaeffler
>
> 'All I know is that it is working and that it's working very well. It's made me think a lot, actually, and I'm not sure we can measure efficiency. ... A lot of what we are doing is different and certainly I haven't been involved in it before' (Roger Evans, Plant Director).
>
> #### Tesco.com
>
> 'So for me it's ... a judgement call based on, "do I feel that I'm getting enough, based on the number of heads I'm employing to do it?"' (Laura Wade-Gery, CEO).

development of effective measures which both incorporate quantitative metrics and also reflect the intangible value that learning processes can generate.

Therefore the development of a range of measures and metrics, appropriate to different stakeholders and for different occasions, is a priority for LTD practitioners. LTD managers need to assure themselves of the continuing and developing operational efficiency of the LTD function. Measures provide the basis through which LTD practitioners can engage with key decision-makers about strategic learning priorities and the extent to which learning can contribute to their achievement. Additionally, measures enable the LTD function to respond positively to any challenges that may be articulated relating to the value contribution that learning is making.

The interviews also highlight the importance of developing measures that are meaningful and relevant for key decision-makers. Therefore, a 'one size fits all' approach is inappropriate. Different metrics and measurement approaches are necessary to take account of different organisational strategies and priorities for learning. Such approaches will utilise a mixture of both 'hard' numerical data and 'soft' qualitative perceptual data.

Four main approaches to assessing the learning value contribution have been identified:

- Learning function efficiency measures are also used by LTD professionals to assess the efficiency and effectiveness of their functional activities.

- Performance against key performance indicators or benchmark standards of 'good practice' or 'excellence'. This approach is adopted frequently and is used by nearly all the organisations in the Value of Learning study.

- Return on investment approaches are the least used, as they are suitable only in limited and specific circumstances.

- Return on expectation measures are more useful to organisations. These assess the extent to which the anticipated benefits of the learning investment have been realised.

BOX 21: HOW MEANINGFUL ARE LEARNING VALUE MEASURES FOR SENIOR MANAGERS?

Canon UK and Ireland

'I think we're fairly attentive as a group to any quantitative analysis of learning issues. We certainly spend a lot of time just thinking about the employee survey type of benchmarking. There is certainly a lot of energy going into analysing those results from every part of the business and not just because we're all paid on that score; but really trying to understand why people feel the way they do' (Matthew Norton, Channel Director).

'Managers in the business like numbers, as in most businesses. They also like talking about softer issues. ... But they're comfortable with numbers. ... They're working with numbers on an everyday basis. So if you give them a number you're speaking their language' (Caroline Price, Strategic Business Partner, HR).

Dublin City Council

'So going back to how meaningful it is, for senior management it's a mark of what's coming out; then ... [we need] to read underneath that, to see if we need to change' (Kathy Quinn, Head of Finance).

The Innovation Group

'I think it all comes down to results. No matter what we say, no matter what we need, it all comes down to results. ... So if we can show the results and the impact of what we've done, then I would expect ... I would insist on spreading that around the rest of the organisation' (Shaun Gwilliam, Software Solutions Director).

Lyreco

'Benchmarking allows you to make the choices in the areas you want to improve because ... it gives you a relative position; ... we can identify which areas we want to concentrate our training and development on. And I would be focusing on the bits that I think would help us win business, or retain business' (Alistair Wood, Logistics Director).

VT plc

'I think our MDs put a lot of store on [metrics], some more than others. I think some just know it is a good thing ... it has face validity, and they say, 'this has got to be good. ... Anything that helps our people to become more effective has got to be good'' (Jo Robbins, HR Director).

These different approaches to measurement are not mutually exclusive and LTD practitioners need to take into account the particular context of their own organisation and to identify a range of measures that are aligned with the particular requirements and strategic priorities of their organisation.

Illustrations of the four different types of measure that emerged are set out fully in Appendix C to this report and shown in summary form in Table 4.

BOX 22: CHALLENGES OF MEASUREMENT

Canon UK and Ireland

'I think the challenge is always: is it the right benchmark? What sits behind that benchmark? So, if you're looking at a benchmark that looks at efficiency, well how effective is it? I don't want to work as part of a learning and development function that is highly efficient but terribly ineffective. So, for me, you can never look at one and not the other. You have to look at both to get the full picture' (Caroline Price, Strategic Business Partner, HR).

'[A challenge is to avoid] forcing some quantitative analysis to the areas that potentially may not yield themselves to do that very efficiently' (Matthew Norton, Channel Director).

Clifford Chance

'People are measuring things so differently: are they taking into account partners' time? … Are they taking into account that lost revenue … of people that are participating?' (Julia Clarke, Global Learning and Development Partner).

VT Group plc

'We have businesses around the world … and all of this data … in itself is very difficult when you are operating in [different parts of the world] and they have a different system. … It's very difficult to get a "wide side" measure' (Jo Robbins, HR Director).

Table 4   Approaches to assessing the learning value contribution

Learning function efficiency measures	Return on expectation measures
Focus on assessing efficiency and effectiveness of the learning function. Although the term 'learning function' is often taken to mean a specialist department, the term can equally well be used in a wider sense to refer to 'the body of Learning and Development activity that has to be provided for an organisation and the people most directly responsible for that provision' (Harrison 2005, p206).	Focus on assessing the extent to which the anticipated benefits of the learning investment have been realised. Key questions underpinning a return on expectation approach are: • What were the original expectations of organisational stakeholders for the learning or training? Have those expectations since changed? • What changes have occurred as a result of the learning processes? • To what extent have stakeholder expectations been met?

Return on investment measures	Key performance indicators and benchmark measures
Focus on an assessment of the benefits of specific learning and training interventions compared with the costs incurred. They may also involve an assessment of the payback period for specific learning or training investments. Key issues here are the extent to which learning is directly contributing to the achievement of defined performance targets.	Focus on the more general evaluation of HR processes and performance through a comparison with key performance indicators or external standards of 'good practice' or 'excellence'. These approaches may be undertaken as a 'one-off' but are more useful when treated as a continuous process in which the organisation continually seeks to challenge and improve its processes.

CONCLUSIONS AND IMPLICATIONS   6

- **A 'one size fits all' approach to value and evaluation is no longer appropriate.**

- **Evaluating the strategic contribution of learning at an organisational level is an ongoing process rather than a singular outcome.**

- **Constructive dialogue with organisational stakeholders is required to underpin the ongoing alignment of learning investments.**

- **An appropriate 'bundle' of measures, incorporating both 'hard' numerical data and 'soft' qualitative information can provide an effective approach to assessing the value of learning.**

INTRODUCTION

This chapter brings together the conclusions which emerged from the semi-structured interviews in the 12 organisations, the online polls and the discussion thread. Additional insights were gained from a literature search. Perhaps the most important conclusion is that the LTD profession needs to adopt new thinking and new practices on the value of learning. The model which is proposed as a result of this study is set out as Figure 6.

A strategic model of value and evaluation is required as organisations recognise that developing and sustaining a strategic approach to learning is necessary to enable them to thrive in a knowledge economy. Although a strategic approach to learning is accepted as necessary, less attention has been paid to the development of organisational measures to assess the contribution that learning is making. This report begins to fill this gap by examining a range of issues related with aligning learning to strategic priorities and establishing and reporting on the strategic value of learning to organisations.

Building on the view that 'value' is defined by the receiver of something, rather than its 'producer', any model of value and evaluation must specifically assess how learning and non-learning stakeholders in contemporary organisations perceive the value of learning and align learning processes with organisational priorities.

THE MODEL OF VALUE AND EVALUATION

It is evident from the earlier discussions that a 'one size fits all' approach to value and evaluation is no longer appropriate. The report has highlighted four factors that influence the development of an appropriate approach for different organisations. These are:

- the level of senior management trust in learning, and the trust other managers place in the contribution of learning to organisational performance

- the extent to which there is an organisational requirement for metrics (and specifically learning value metrics) to underpin decision-making processes in the organisation

- the importance of short-term capability requirements for the strategic success of the organisation

- the importance of long-term capability requirements for the strategic success of the organisation.

Every organisation is different, and the approach required to assess the learning value contribution will depend on the individual 'mix' of characteristics. All four factors are relevant for LTD practitioners to take into account although, depending on the particular context of the organisation, some will be more significant than others. In addition, organisational characteristics and capability requirements may change over time. The measurement of value, therefore, is a process as much as an outcome; it involves:

- determining the current alignment of learning processes against the organisation's strategic priorities

- identifying a range of methods to assess and evaluate the contribution that learning is making

- establishing, through dialogue with senior decision-makers, the most relevant approaches to value and evaluation for the organisation.

Working from the basis that 'value' is contextual, the model

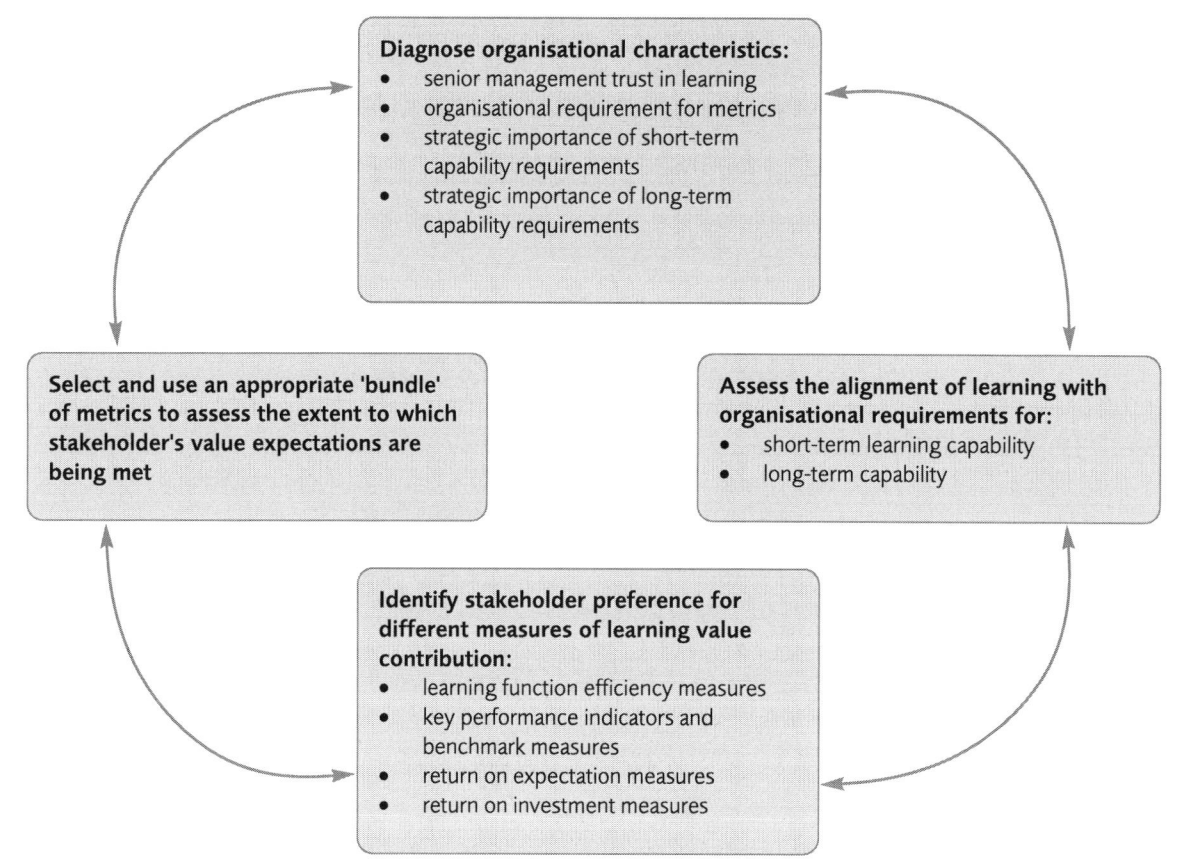

CONCLUSIONS AND IMPLICATIONS

Figure 6 A model of value and evaluation

Diagnose organisational characteristics:
- senior management trust in learning
- organisational requirement for metrics
- strategic importance of short-term capability requirements
- strategic importance of long-term capability requirements

Select and use an appropriate 'bundle' of metrics to assess the extent to which stakeholder's value expectations are being met

Assess the alignment of learning with organisational requirements for:
- short-term learning capability
- long-term capability

Identify stakeholder preference for different measures of learning value contribution:
- learning function efficiency measures
- key performance indicators and benchmark measures
- return on expectation measures
- return on investment measures

indicates the importance of taking account of the expectations of key stakeholders in any strategic approach to value and evaluation. This involves identifying the expectations of the contribution learning can make to the organisation from the perspective of organisational stakeholders rather than focusing on the functional preferences of trainers. Organisational stakeholders expect learning to add value to two interconnected aspects of performance. First, learning is expected to contribute to the efficiency of operational and organisational 'infrastructure' processes. Second, it is expected to contribute to the ability of the organisation to achieve strategic differentiation.

Learning processes are particularly valued by key stakeholders when they can be shown to contribute to:

- the 'strategic readiness' of employees
- the delivery of performance improvement
- the delivery of cost-effective labour
- career/talent-management processes.

The report also highlights how the expectations of senior operational managers and LTD executives about what learning can contribute may differ. There is, therefore, a need for a constructive dialogue between LTD practitioners and line managers through which challenging and achievable expectations for the learning contribution to the organisation can be agreed.

Ensuring that investment in learning is aligned with strategic priorities is an important feature of the value and evaluation process. Constructive dialogue between LTD practitioners and key organisational stakeholders is essential because learning activities may well be funded through a variety of different budgets. Effective learning requires agreement to invest in the time needed to learn as well as financial support.

LTD involvement in business planning and review processes is an important way for alignment to be achieved and maintained. Organisational key performance indicators provide a useful basis for assessing the extent to which ongoing alignment is being achieved, particularly for organisations where short-term capability requirements are of strategic significance. External or sectoral benchmark measures provide another way of assessing alignment, particularly for organisations where longer-term capability issues are vital.

FROM RETURN ON INVESTMENT TO RETURN ON EXPECTATION

The effective assessment of the value contribution made by learning involves making use of qualitative (softer) types of information as well as quantitative, numerically based, metrics.

The report has identified four different approaches to assessing the value of learning:

- learning function efficiency measures
- key performance indicators and benchmark measures
- return on investment measures
- return on expectation measures.

It is important that LTD professionals measure and monitor the operational efficiency of the learning function. However, the report suggests that other organisational stakeholders do not use learning function efficiency measures as a basis for evaluating the contribution that learning makes to the organisation. In some cases human capital measures that focus on organisational achievement against key performance indicators and benchmarks are more relevant for senior managers.

Return on Investment measures, for so long considered to be the 'holy grail' for LTD professionals, are of limited interest to senior decision-makers. The report highlights how attention is shifting from return on investment to return on expectation measures of value. Return on expectation measures make use of both 'hard' and 'soft' information and assess the extent to which the anticipated benefits of the learning investment have been realised.

Key questions underpinning a return on expectation approach are:

- What were the original expectations of organisational stakeholders for the learning or training? Have those expectations since changed?
- What changes have occurred as a result of the learning processes?
- To what extent have stakeholder expectations been met?

LTD practitioners should, therefore, select and use an appropriate bundle of metrics that will enable them to assess and communicate to stakeholders the extent to which their value expectations are being met.

IMPLICATIONS FOR LTD PRACTITIONERS

The report has identified a number of areas for the development of practice within the LTD profession.

LTD practitioners and senior managers who wish to review their approach to the value and evaluation process may find that the questions used for the Value of Learning project semi-structured interviews offer a useful way to review current practice:

- How does the learning function provide strategic value to your organisation?
- How will the learning function's strategic activity translate into business results?
- What is the learning investment process and your involvement in it?
- How do you know the learning function is maintaining ongoing alignment with your organisation's strategic business needs?
- How do you measure the learning function's value contribution to your organisation today?
- How do you know that the learning function is functioning as efficiently as possible?
- How do you measure and report on value?

Additionally, effective value and evaluation processes require practitioners to:

- Focus on the strategic capability requirements of their organisation rather than on their functional preferences.
- Work proactively with senior decision-makers to develop management trust in the learning value contribution and to identify the extent to which stakeholders require qualitative and/or quantitative measures of the value of learning.
- Identify a balanced range of aggregate human-capital-related measures that are significant for the organisation in its specific context.
- Engage in constructive dialogue with organisational stakeholders to establish value expectations for learning.
- Go beyond learning function efficiency measures. These are important to reassure the organisation that the function is working effectively but they are not sufficient as measures of the strategic value of learning for the organisation.
- Develop and use measures of value and evaluation that are relevant to organisational stakeholders, strategic priorities and context. Measures of return on expectation, rather than return on investment, are more likely to meet these needs.

APPENDIX A
THE RESEARCH PROJECT

In November 2006 the CIPD appointed members of the University of Portsmouth Business School to undertake the Value of Learning research project. The research was exploratory in purpose, aiming to establish how practitioners and senior decision-makers perceive the value of learning and how organisations are measuring and demonstrating its strategic value to the organisation as a whole.

PROJECT OBJECTIVES

The specific research objectives were:

- to examine how learning and non-learning stakeholders in contemporary organisations perceive the value of learning

- to investigate how organisations currently report on value and to establish specifically what metrics of business and human capital performance are found to be most valuable

- to develop a framework of value and evaluation through which practitioners can assess and enhance the value of learning to organisational and individual performance.

DATA COLLECTION

Following an initial literature review, data were gathered from three sources:

- contributions to a CIPD Value of Learning online discussion thread

- responses to two Value of Learning online polls hosted on the CIPD website

- separate semi-structured interviews undertaken on a 'matched pair' basis with a senior operational manager and an LTD executive in 12 organisations.

RESEARCH DESIGN

The research took into account a previous study by the American Society of Training and Development (ASTD) into the extent to which perceptions of the strategic value of learning held by senior learning professionals were aligned with those of their chief executives (O'Driscoll et al 2005). The research design for the CIPD project built on and extended the methods used in the ASTD study to make possible an examination of further features of the value and evaluation process as it is developing in UK organisations.

An incremental approach to the research process, which commenced in November 2006, was adopted as follows:

1. Invitation to CIPD Virtual Trainers Network to contribute to the Value of Learning online discussion thread.

2. The construction of questions for the first Value of Learning online poll was informed by issues emerging from contributions to the online discussion thread, as well as from the literature about value and evaluation.

3. The questions for the semi-structured interviews replicated those used in semi-structured interviews for the ASTD study.

4. The construction of questions for the second Value of Learning online poll was informed by further issues emerging from the online discussion thread and from themes emerging from initial analysis of early semi-structured interviews.

The research population for the online discussion thread and the online polls comprised all members of the CIPD Virtual Trainers Network (3,500 people). The discussion thread was opened on 13 November 2006; by 4 July 2007 the site had received 1,436 visits and 45 contributions had been made.

There were 392 responses to the first online poll, which ran from

December 2006 to the end of January 2007. The second poll, which ran from February to the end of March 2007, had 244 usable responses (technical issues affected a further 56 responses which were discounted for analysis purposes). The poll questions and a summary of the responses are shown as Appendix B.

A purposive approach to sampling was adopted for the semi-structured interviews to ensure a geographical representation of organisations (within UK and Ireland) and also to ensure the inclusion of different types and sizes of organisation. Twenty organisations were approached and it was possible to achieve face-to-face interviews with both a senior operational manager and the most senior person responsible for LTD in 12 of them. Interviews took place between January and April 2007. The participating organisations are shown in Table A1

INTERVIEW PROCESS AND PROTOCOL

Separate interviews were held with a senior operational manager or executive and with the most senior person responsible for LTD in each organisation. Interviewees were given the same advance briefing and the same questions were asked in each case. Interviewees in the same organisation were asked not to work together to prepare a 'corporate response' and were reassured that the purpose of the research was to find out about their perceptions and emerging practice. Interviewees were reassured that there were no 'right answers' and responses in their own words about what they really thought in response to the questions asked would be valued. Interviews were all tape-recorded (with permission) and transcribed for later analysis. The questions that were asked are shown in Chapter 1 (Box 2).

DATA ANALYSIS

Each interview transcript was read independently by two researchers. Each researcher independently identified recurring themes from within the transcripts. Themes were compared and a common set was selected. This approach to initial analysis enabled the identification of some 'overarching' themes that emerged from responses to all of the questions asked in the interviews. Other themes that were relevant to specific questions were also identified in this way. The themes were then used as a basis for coding and analysis using the NVivo7 qualitative data analysis software. The same themes were utilised for content analysis of the contributions to the CIPD online discussion thread.

ETHICS

The research was undertaken in accordance with the ethical guidelines of the University of Portsmouth Business School.

DISSEMINATION

Interim findings from the research were used to inform the development of a CIPD Value of Learning online tool and a CIPD Value of Learning Change Agenda document (2007c, 2007d), both of which were published in April 2007.

Table A1 — Semi-structured interviews: participating organisations

Organisation	Size	Type	Location of interviews	LTD interviewee	Senior management interviewee
Canon UK and Ireland	Large	Private sector	England	Strategic Business Partner (HR)	Channel Director
Christian Aid	Medium	Not-for-profit	England	Head of Learning and Development	Chief Executive Officer
Clifford Chance	Large	Partnership	England	Global Learning and Development Partner	Senior Partner
Dublin City Council	Large	Public sector	Ireland	Training Manager	Head of Finance
The Football Association	Medium	Not-for-profit	England	Learning and Development Manager	Director of Corporate Affairs
Glasgow Housing Association	Medium	Not-for-profit	Scotland	Learning and Development Manager	Acting CEO
The Innovation Group plc	Medium	Private sector	England	Training Manager	Software Solutions Director
Lyreco UK Ltd	Large	Private sector	England	Training and Development Director	Logistics Director
The National Audit Office	Large	Public sector	England	Director of Development and Employment	Deputy Comptroller and Auditor General
Schaeffler UK Ltd	Medium	Private sector	Wales	Human Resources Director	Plant Director
Tesco.com	Large	Private sector	England	Personnel Director	Chief Executive Officer
VT Group plc	Large	Private sector	England	Group HR Director	Chief Executive Officer

APPENDIX B
ONLINE POLL RESULTS AND SUMMARIES

The results and summaries produced here were first published on the CIPD website (http://www.cipd.co.uk/helpingpeoplelearn).

FIRST VALUE OF LEARNING ONLINE POLL

Introduction

Based on current academic and practitioner work and also the Value of Learning discussion thread results, we produced a poll investigating the barriers to evaluating learning and invited network members to participate online. In all, 392 CIPD members contributed during the period November 2006 to January 2007.

The poll results are given in Table A2, and are interesting in terms of the extent to which respondents perceived different barriers when taken in relation to one another (as reflected in the combined 'always/very often' total shown in the right-hand column). The two propositions which had the highest level of agreement related to evaluation being too costly given other priorities, and the lack of interest from line managers in evaluation. The lowest level of support was given to the proposition concerning poor learning objectives as a barrier to evaluating learning.

Comments on the results

The poll results reflected the concerns expressed in the discussion thread. While 'unclear learning objectives' was the barrier to learning rated lowest, at 37 per cent, this may not be something the LTD practitioner can easily affect given that the lack of clarity may come either from the line manager or the learners themselves.

Around half the respondents reported 'lack of effective techniques' as a barrier to learning evaluation. The discussion thread also suggested that while Kirkpatrick Levels 1 and 2 can be undertaken, measuring at higher levels is problematic. Indeed some respondents appeared to doubt the possibility of providing any adequate measure, identifying 'benefits are too difficult to measure' as a barrier (60 per cent). This finding presents food for thought in terms of the potential for developing a measure in the future. Clearly any measure would need to be convincing to a wide range of stakeholders.

The apparent lack of influence from evaluation processes on future decisions was considered a barrier to evaluation by 53 per cent of respondents. This suggests that decisions about LTD may not be influenced by any evaluation outcomes. This is being probed in the current stage of the project, which involves interviews with both learning and non-learning decision-makers in organisations. We are also examining the influence of the cost of evaluation, which was seen by 57 per cent as a barrier within the first poll.

The propositions with the highest level of agreement highlight the importance of developing time-effective evaluation practices which are relevant to the needs and priorities of managers.

SECOND VALUE OF LEARNING ONLINE POLL

Introduction

This is the second poll in the Value of Learning project. It focused on key issues located in the literature about evaluation, early interviews undertaken as part of the project and the Value of Learning discussion thread.

Results

The poll was open between February and March 2007 and there were 244 complete responses. The results are shown in Table A3 below. The initial analysis has grouped the first two columns into a generalised 'agree' score for each proposition (in the right-hand column).

POLL RESULTS AND SUMMARIES

Table A2 Poll results of first online poll

Please indicate on this poll the barriers that you have experienced with 'serious' evaluation of learning and training in your organisation:

Proposition	Always	Very often	Sometimes	Never	Total of 'Always' + 'Very often'
The objectives of learning and training interventions are unclear	8.7%	27.9%	51.1%	11.1%	37%
We lack effective evaluation techniques	15.6%	35.5%	37.4%	10.3%	51%
Decisions about future learning and training are not influenced by the results of training evaluation processes	17.2%	36.3%	35.9%	10.3%	53%
The organisation is more concerned to measure the costs and not the benefits of learning and training	20.2%	36.6%	31.7%	11.1%	57%
The benefits of learning and training interventions are too difficult to measure	14.1%	45.8%	35.9%	3.4%	60%
Line managers are not interested in training evaluation; they do not or would not use the data	19.1%	47.0%	29.0%	4.6%	66%
Serious evaluation is too time consuming/costly and we have other priorities	22.5%	47.3%	24.8%	5.3%	70%

Several propositions cluster at over 80 per cent agreement. One of these concerned the importance of learning for all employees, a view that supports other CIPD evidence about the development from training to learning in modern organisations. Line managers were seen as a key stakeholder group for the evaluation of learning by more than 80 per cent of the group. Interestingly, although more than 70 per cent of respondents supported the use of return on investment (ROI) as a method of evaluating learning, more than 80 per cent thought that senior managers would be less concerned about metrics if they developed a trusting relationship with LTD professionals.

Two propositions attracted lower support from respondents. One of these concerned the reliance on metrics to determine the value of learning. The other proposition receiving less support was that job competence rather than the development of individuals' potential should be the learning focus.

Comments on the results

The poll results reflect the debate on the discussion thread and our Value of Learning project interviews with senior practitioners regarding the challenges of evaluating the contribution of learning. One aspect which surfaced was 'value for whom?' Line managers (rather than senior managers) were perceived by respondents as key stakeholders in the evaluation of learning. However, senior management trust in the LTD function is important if investment in learning is to be achieved and maintained. Value of learning interviews (currently being completed) may shed light on this process and the ways in which LTD activity can be aligned to the needs of participants, their line managers and senior managers.

The poll results also highlight the importance of the timescale of value from learning activities. Over 80 per cent of respondents indicated a concern with developing individual potential (inferring longer-term investment) as well as meeting the shorter-term job-related competence needs of the organisation. How to manage this process in fast-moving environments is now a major theme within our research.

In addition, the poll results also contribute to the debate about the use of metrics. Results from the first Value of Learning poll suggested that finding effective and time-efficient metrics is a challenge for practitioners. This second poll suggests that a minority of respondents would want to 'rely on metrics'. Our initial Value of Learning case studies suggest that the level of significance of ROI and other metrics may depend on different organisational contexts.

VALUE OF LEARNING

Table A3 — Poll results of second online poll

Please indicate on this poll your opinions about these propositions on evaluating the contribution of learning:

Proposition	Agree	Mostly agree	Mostly disagree	Disagree	Total who Agree or Mostly agree
Balancing the need to invest learning resources in addressing short-term issues as well as longer-term learning needs is a challenge in my organisation	30.5%	51.4%	15.6%	2.0%	82%
Providing learning opportunities for all employees is an important part of the management style of my organisation	45.2%	38.2%	13.9%	2.4%	83%
Managers understand the cost and value of training activities rather than the contribution of learning to the organisation	12.3%	51.0%	32.5%	4.1%	63%
Senior managers will be less concerned about value of learning metrics if they have developed a relationship of trust with the LTD function	22.2%	58.8%	15.6%	2.0%	81%
Statistical measures should be used to establish the return on investment (ROI) of learning activities	14.8%	59.2%	22.6%	3.2%	74%
Investment in learning in the organisation should be focused on achieving job-related competence rather than developing individuals' potential	4.5%	33.7%	51.4%	9.8%	38%
I would like my organisation to rely on metrics to determine the value of learning	2.0%	36.2%	51.0%	8.6%	38%
Line managers rather than senior managers are the key stakeholders when evaluating learning	32.0%	50.6%	14.8%	2.4%	83%

The Value of Learning polls and the summary results were written by Professor Charlotte Rayner, Portsmouth Business School.

APPENDIX C
EXAMPLES OF MEASUREMENT OPTIONS

The measurement options indicated here were first published as part of the CIPD Value of Learning online tool (http://www.cipd.co.uk/subjects/training/trneval/_vlulrngtl.htm).

Learning function efficiency measures

What matters to the organisation?	Measurement option(s) (for different staff groups)
Is the learning function delivering operational effectiveness?	<ul><li>Training days per employee</li><li>Off-the-job training days (FTE)</li><li>Training spend as a percentage of salary bill</li><li>Proportion of staff with personal development plans</li></ul>
How effectively is the functional capability of the workforce being developed?	<ul><li>Organisational skills profile</li><li>Organisational qualifications profile</li><li>Proportion of staff deemed at acceptable level of competence or above</li><li>Proportion of hires from within compared with externally sourced</li></ul>
How well are learning interventions supporting our critical success factors?	<ul><li>Types of learning and development available – take-up of opportunities – comparison of types of training and development available against organisational key performance indicators</li></ul>
How does our investment in learning compare with that of other relevant organisations?	<ul><li>Spend on learning and training compared with relevant benchmark data about spending patterns</li></ul>
To what extent is learning contributing to the organisation's flexibility and 'change agility'?	<ul><li>Qualitative assessment data (eg focus groups; feedback from managers)</li><li>Succession planning or career planning data - how many people prepared for next career move?</li></ul>

EXAMPLES OF MEASUREMENT OPTIONS

Key performance indicators and benchmark measures

What matters to the organisation?	Measurement option(s) (for different staff groups)
How does our organisational performance compare with that of other relevant organisations?	• Performance comparisons with relevant benchmark data, eg – revenue per employee – profit per employee – sales per employee
To what extent are we developing an appropriate psychological contract with our employees?	• Employee satisfaction data (qualitative and quantitative)
Are our employees developing in line with the emerging needs of the organisation?	• Development review data (appraisal-based) mapped against organisational strategy • Management feedback
To what extent are our operational key performance indicators and business process efficiency objectives and targets being met?	• Data on achievement of learning and development initiatives contributing to business process efficiency targets and objectives
To what extent are employees able to apply what they learn at work to the benefit of the organisation?	• Learner survey data • Management survey data • Appraisal data on performance ratings

Return on investment measures

What matters to the organisation?	Measurement option(s) (for different staff groups)
How is learning contributing directly to the achievement of our organisational targets?	• Time-to-competence data • Proportion of employees with required competence level • Customer feedback data • Employee engagement data • Number of individuals able to move into key positions
To what extent are employees achieving their performance targets?	• Achievement against performance appraisal targets
How cost-effective are the learning and training opportunities we provide?	• Employee reaction and learning data (level 1 and 2 evaluation) • Management feedback data
What economic benefits does our investment in training provide?	• Cost-benefit data for specific learning interventions
Is learning contributing directly to the achievement of HR targets?	• Performance data on relevant HR targets, eg – absence – retention – number of internal promotions

VALUE OF LEARNING

Return on expectation measures

What matters to the organisation?	Measurement option(s) (for different staff groups)
To what extent are employees learning to exhibit the behavioural competences that we require?	• Management survey data • Employee attitude survey data
How successfully are we able to manage succession and talent pool issues?	• Numbers of staff covered by succession planning process • Size of relevant talent pool • Achievement against succession action plan • Exit interview data
To what extent are we equipped with the people skills needed to mitigate risks to achieving our strategic objectives?	• Management survey data • Operational risk analysis
To what extent are learning and growth objectives and targets being met?	• Data on achievement against learning and growth targets and objectives

How does our people performance compare with that of other relevant organisations?	• Performance comparisons with relevant benchmark data, eg
	  – customer satisfaction
	  – customer loyalty
	  – supplier relationships

REFERENCES

ACCENTURE (2004) *High-performance workforce study.* http://www.cpp.com/pr/accenture.pdf [accessed 18 May 2007].

BECKER, G. (1964) *Human capital.* New York: National Bureau of Economic Research.

BRAMLEY, P. (2003) *Evaluating training.* London: CIPD.

BRYANS, P. and SMITH, R. (2000) Beyond training: reconceptualising learning at work. *Journal of Workplace Learning.* Vol. 12, No. 6. pp228–235.

BURROW, J. and BERARDINELLI, P. (2003) Systematic performance improvement: refining the space between learning and results. *Journal of Workplace Learning.* Vol. 15, No. 1. pp6–13.

CHARTERED INSTITUTE OF PERSONNEL AND DEVELOPMENT (2005a) *Training to learning.* Change Agenda. Online version available at: http://www.cipd.co.uk/subjects/lrnanddev/general/train2lrn0405.htm [accessed 15 February 2007].

CHARTERED INSTITUTE OF PERSONNEL AND DEVELOPMENT (2005b) *Who learns at work? Employees experiences of training and development, Survey Report.* March. Online version available at: http://www.cipd.co.uk/subjects/training/general/learnatwk.htm?IsSrchRes=1 [accessed 25 August 2007].

CHARTERED INSTITUTE OF PERSONNEL AND DEVELOPMENT (2006a) *Learning and development annual survey report 2006.* Online version available at: http://www.cipd.co.uk/NR/rdonlyres/97BE272C-8859-4DB1-BD99-17F38E4B4484/0/lrnandevsurv0406.pdf [accessed 18 May 2007].

CHARTERED INSTITUTE OF PERSONNEL AND DEVELOPMENT (2006b) *The value of learning: a discussion paper.* Online version available at: http://www.cipd.co.uk/helpingpeoplelearn/_valoflrning.htm [accessed 23 May 2007].

CHARTERED INSTITUTE OF PERSONNEL AND DEVELOPMENT (2006c) *What's the future for human capital?* London: CIPD.

CHARTERED INSTITUTE OF PERSONNEL AND DEVELOPMENT (2007a) *Learning and development, annual survey report.* Online version available at: http://www.cipd.co.uk/subjects/lrnanddev/general/_lrngdevsvy.htm?IsSrchRes=1 [accessed 25 August 2007].

CHARTERED INSTITUTE OF PERSONNEL AND DEVELOPMENT (2007b) *Learning and the line: the role of line managers in training, learning and development.* Change Agenda. Online version available at: http://www.cipd.co.uk/subjects/maneco/general/_lrngln.htm [accessed 23 August 2007].

CHARTERED INSTITUTE OF PERSONNEL AND DEVELOPMENT (2007c) *The value of learning: a new model of value and evaluation.* Change Agenda. Online version available at http://www.cipd.co.uk/subjects/training/trneval/_vlrngnwmdl.htm [accessed 18 September 2007].

REFERENCES

CHARTERED INSTITUTE OF PERSONNEL AND DEVELOPMENT (2007d) *Value of Learning: Assessing and reporting on the value of learning to your organisation.* Tool. Online version available at: http://www.cipd.co.uk/subjects/training/trneval/_vlulrngtl.htm [accessed 18 September 2007].

DIONNE, P. (1996) The evaluation of training activities: a complex issue involving different stakes. *Human Resource Development Quarterly.* Vol. 7, No. 3. pp279–286.

FITZ-ENZ, J. (2000) *ROI of human capital: measuring the economic value of employee performance.* New York: Amacon.

HARRISON, R. (2005) *Learning and development.* London: CIPD.

HUSELID, M., JACKSON, S.E. and SCHULER, R. (1997) Technical and strategic human resources management effectiveness as determinants of firm performance. *Academy of Management Journal.* Vol. 40, No. 1. pp171–189.

JOHNS, T. (2005), Foreword to Rayner, C. and Adam-Smith, D. (eds) *Managing and leading people.* London: CIPD.

KAPLAN, R.S. and NORTON, D.P. (1992) The balanced scorecard: measures that drive performance. *Harvard Business Review.* Vol. 70, No. 1. pp75–85.

KEARNS, P. (2005) *Evaluating the ROI from learning.* London: CIPD.

KIRKPATRICK, D. (1975) *Evaluating training programs.* Alexandria, Va.: American Society of Training and Development.

NICKOLS, F.W. (2005) Why a stakeholder approach to evaluating learning. *Advances in Developing Human Resources.* Vol. 7, No. 1. p123.

O'DRISCOLL, T. (2005) *Valuing human capital and HRD: a new millennium requires a new approach.* Unpublished report.

O'DRISCOLL, T., SUGRUE, B. and VONA, M.K. (2005). The C level and the value of learning. *Training and Development.* October. pp70–75.

PFEFFER, J. (1998) *The human equation: building profits by putting people first.* Boston, Mass.: Harvard Business School Press

PHILLIPS, J (1998) Systematic evaluation: trends and practices. In J. Phillips (ed) *Implementing evaluation systems and processes,* Alexandria, Va.: American Society for Training and Development.

PURCELL, J., HUTCHINSON S., KINNIE, N., RAYTON, B. and SWART. J. (2003) *Understanding the people and performance link: unlocking the black box.* London: CIPD.

RUSS-EFT, D. and PRESKILL, H. (2001) *Evaluation in organisations.* Cambridge: Perseus.

SADLER-SMITH, E., DOWN, S. and FIELD, J. (1999) Adding value to HRD: evaluation, investors in people and small firm training. *Human Resource Development International.* Vol. 2, No. 4. pp369–390.

SCARBOROUGH, H. and ELIAS, J. (2002) *Evaluating human capital,* London: CIPD.

SCHULTZ, T.W. (1961) Investments in human capital. *American Economic Review.* Vol. 51, No. 1. pp1–17.

SLOMAN, M. (2007) *The changing world of the trainer.* Oxford: Butterworth Heinemann.

SUGRUE, B. and KIM, K. (2004) *American Society of Training and Development (ASTD) state of the industry report.* Alexandria Va.: American Society for Training and Development.

SUGRUE, B., O'DRISCOLL, T. and VONA, M.K. (2006) *C level perceptions of the strategic value of learning research report,* Alexandria Va.: American Society for Training and Development and IBM.

THOMSON, I. (2007) *Evaluation of training.* Chartered Institute of Personnel and Development (CIPD) factsheet. On-line version available at: http://www.cipd.co.uk/subjects/training/trneval/evatrain.htm [accessed 18 May 2007].

ULRICH, D. and BROCKBANK, W. (2005) *The HR Value Proposition.* Boston, Mass.: Harvard Business School Press.